The All-Purpose Knots Bible

[3 in 1] The Step-by-Step Illustrated Guide to Learn How to Tie 150 Vital Knots for All Needs | For Camping, Hunting & Bushcraft Included

Conrad Fowler

TABLE OF CONTENTS

INTRODUCTION

In today's hectic environment, we frequently seek out hobbies to help us relieve some of the stress we are under. Many people ignore this crucial component since we are preoccupied with pursuing our goals and desires. We neglect to take action to relieve the stress that has built up due to our stressful activities, especially at work.

People frequently miss hobbies for various reasons, including lack of money, reluctance to learn something new, etc. In my experience, I used to be like way, and I didn't have any hobbies because I didn't want to pick up new skills. I'm glad a friend introduced me to the pastime of "knot tying." Since you are just sitting there tying ropes, I initially thought it was boring and never imagined I would become addicted to this pastime.

But I was mistaken, as this pastime is quite entertaining and allows you to produce a variety of knot patterns that will satisfy you and make the experience unique. All of my tension has decreased since I learned how to tie knots, especially when I do it after work.

I practiced knot-tying after work every day after learning the various approaches, which is how I perfected it. I feel privileged to impart my knot-tying expertise to you through this book. You will undoubtedly love working on the knot-tying tasks in this book because they are highly beginner-friendly.

The projects we'll work on can be advanced once you've mastered them by including changes that suit your preferences. Do not worry; it is common for you to struggle with some of the concepts we are covering initially. Similar to when I first started, there were some tying positions and techniques that I did not understand until I gave them a lot of practice and eventually mastered them.

I advise against going all out on a certain project. Before moving on to the following phase, you must be comfortable with the previous step to master the skills. If you constantly follow the steps exactly, I can assure you that it will be challenging and that you will struggle to complete a different job with the same processes the next time you confront a different job with the same processes.

The next time you come into that tying, you will undoubtedly not have a difficult time; thus, you can do it effortlessly if you learn to control every step of your heart. To fully comprehend the modules, I can only encourage you to take an interest in doing this and internalize the content.

It makes no difference if you have sewing experience because it is irrelevant. This book will undoubtedly teach you a lot of stuff.

We should not put off our education, and therefore let's go to work on the projects.

BOOK 1

Knots for Beginners

INTRODUCTION

When you think about the first time you tied the knot, you will probably not be able to pinpoint exactly when. Knots have always been in our lives, from the simplest act of tying our shoes, tying a tie, and tying hair ribbons to more complicated actions such as fastening a fishing line or securing a load.

Let us now look at a brief history of knot-tying:

CHAPTER 1

KNOTTING HISTORY

What is Knotting?

Knotting secures or fastens linear material—specifically rope—by interweaving and tying. Sometimes, one length of rope is used, and other times, several lengths are used. When a rope is not the main item in use, chains, straps, twine, or other forms of webbing could also be used so that they could come together and may even be able to anchor themselves to "loads" or, in other words, other objects.

Knots have been used since ancient times and are mostly used by rescue professionals, arborists, scouts, climbers, and sailors. For one, if you want to gain the mechanical advantage or if you want to have makeshift tools with you, knots can help. You can also use knots to transport items—the way levers or zip lines work. Sometimes, they can also be used for decorative purposes. They can be used for many things, so some people believe more people should know how to make some knots. The International Guild of Knot Tiers aims to promote the art of knot-tying worldwide.

Brief History of Knot Tying

When we look back, the most primitive remains of knots and ropes date back to approximately 15,000-17,000 years ago. This suggests that knotting technology is more ancient than the ax or wheel. Knots have existed through time as a crucial component for significant innovations such as basket-making, hunting traps, and fishing nets.

How Were Knots Used in The Past?

Before planes, trains, subways, and cars, transportation used animals or boats. It was necessary to secure the boats on the dock to avoid them being drawn away by a powerful tide. Also, the animals were tied up to prevent them from wandering off. At the time, fastening a knot meant holding on to something valuable or losing it.

The most commonly utilized knot for securing boats was the bowline knot, and it dates back to the Egyptian era based on the fossils from recently excavated ships. With time, people have discovered several hundred knots that range from easy knots that you can create within a second to more convoluted ones which call for step-by-step directions.

We have seen how this skill was invaluable in the past, so how about we go through the usefulness of knot-tying in our contemporary society?

Below are the various ways that we now use this practice:

Practical Applications of Knot Tying

Knot tying can be used in the following situations:

1. Knots are instrumental for carrying out outdoor activities such as:
    - ✓ Mountaineering
    - ✓ Camping- e.g., making some camping tools and setting up tents
    - ✓ Hunting
    - ✓ Sailing/boating/seamanship/ canoeing

2. Knots are also frequently utilized in arts and crafts; the most common instance is macramé. Macramé grew as a primary craft during the 1970s. Examples of the most popular knots in macramé are the overhand knot, clove hitch, spiral stitch, square knot, and lark's head knot.
3. Truckers utilize the trucker's hitch to gain a mechanical advantage when securing a load.
4. You can also use this skill in making makeshift tools: the munter hitch, which you can utilize in fastening, and the bowline knot, which works as a rescue loop.
5. You can further apply knot making in forming a high line, nearly identical to the zip line, which can be utilized in moving injured people, supplies, or inexperienced people across ravines, crevices, or rivers.

1. *It is worth remembering that the systems described above generally call for using various suitable knots tied appropriately.
2. *You may also combine knots to create intricate items like netting and lanyards.

CHAPTER 2

FUNDAMENTALS OF KNOTS

Every rope and knot is made in a certain way. Ropes, string, and yarn all have many pieces that make up the final product. Anatomy explains how these pieces work together, while taxonomy is the process of classifying these pieces. The following words are important to knot-making because they classify items or work together in a specific way.

Fiber

Traditionally, fiber is a naturally occurring product. It contains organic material from cotton, manila, and hemp. The fibers are woven to create ropes. However, naturally occurring products often disintegrate over time, so ropes from natural fibers may become mildewed or even rot. Natural ropes also become weaker in water. Yet, natural fibers remain popular for rope making.

Synthetic fibers are made from manufactured materials. These materials include polyesters, nylon, and acrylics. Synthetic fibers are woven in the same way as their natural counterparts. But synthetic fibers are much stronger, especially under tension. Synthetic fibers might be slippery and are frequently damaged by ultraviolet light.

Yarn

A length of fiber is called yarn. Yarn is a long string of fibers that link together to form strands. Yarn is found in fabric, ropes, knitting, and many other places. Cotton is the most common fiber for yarn, but synthetic polyester is also popular. Some yarns are a combination of fibers. The yarn type can help determine whether a specific rope is best for your activities.

Strand

A strand is a length of interconnected yarn fibers, and the yarn connects by plaiting, twisting, or lying next to each other.

A strand is similar to a single hair or piece of thread - it consists of several small pieces that form a larger object. Ropes contain many threads, which can come loose. This loosening is called fraying or unraveling. All the threads together form a strand, such as in a single length of rope or string.

Rope

A rope is formed when strands of yarn are woven together. The massive number of strands in a rope makes it strong and useful for many activities. Ropes often consist of several strands twisted or braided together. This structure gives ropes extra strength and helps the fibers to stay together. Any tension on the rope is spread across the different strands, which creates tensile strength. Ropes can be made from synthetic or natural materials.

Line

A line is a single length of thin material. A familiar example is the fishing line. A line is usually made from synthetic materials and comes in various colors. Knots are important for lines as they help secure the lines' pieces. A smooth, slippery line can break when there is too much tension.

Hawser

A hawser is a thick rope or cable. It is normally used on ships to help with towing or mooring. A hawsehole, commonly called a cat hole, is the opening on a ship through which the hawser passes. Hawsers help hoist and move ships, so they must be very thick for extra strength.

Cable

A cable is a very strong rope that can be quite heavy. The purpose of the cable determines what it is made of. For example, climbing cables are made from synthetic materials, hawsers are made from natural fibers, and other stronger cables may have woven metal strands. Some cables have long strands of woven fibers, called a core, covered with a sheath coating, usually made from plastic or other woven fibers.

Safety and General Guidelines

Working safely with ropes is important. Any activity has risks, and a person can get hurt; knot tying is no different. Frequently working with ropes can lead to rashes or scrapes on your hands, which can be painful. Sometimes, people cut themselves or fall if a knot is not secured properly to an object. Maintain proper safety when tying knots and always ask a parent for help if you are still a child.

Basic Rope and Knot Safety

Many sports, hobbies, and activities use knots, but you must be careful while working with equipment. Any rope or line activity has its risks. Poor handling, an incorrect grip, and weak knots pose dangers. Always check that your equipment is safe to use before and during the process.

Rope Strength

Every rope or line has maximum strength. The load factor, sometimes called the design factor, indicates the rope's strength. The higher the load factor, the stronger the rope. You cannot lift a heavy object with a weak rope, so keep that in mind when selecting a rope. Some ropes experience sudden loads, such as tugging, which requires a greater load factor. Never overload a rope. Any rope is fine if you are learning to make knots. However, do not use the same rope to lift, pull, or lower any item. Rather, research to find the rope best suited for your activities. Some ropes are heat-sensitive or become weaker in water, so check these things before purchasing a rope. Ropes should be kept clean as dirt infiltrates and weakens the fibers. Chemicals and sunlight damage ropes, so do not leave a rope lying in the sun or near abrasive substances.

Knots and Imperfections Reduce Rope Strength

Any flaw in a rope makes it weaker. A rope is at its strongest when used in its original form. Scuff marks, weak fibers, and imperfections can weaken a rope. Any kinks or knots significantly reduce a rope's strength.

Remember to use a suitable rope that is stronger than your minimum requirements. Sometimes, brand-new ropes have imperfections, resulting in weakness, so check your equipment properly before using it. Any knot or kink in a rope must be removed before packing it.

Keep Your Limbs Out of the Way

Always check where a rope or line is when doing knot work. Never stand near a bight or loop because a sudden tightening may cause the rope to catch your legs. Do not walk over a rope or try to balance on it. Some people think they will get a better grip by wrapping a rope around their hand, but this is unsafe. Do not wrap anything around your fingers, hands, or arms, as it can disrupt circulation, cut you, or, in extreme cases, sever limbs. Please do not make sudden movements when working with rope or line because it may cause unexpected reactions that will hurt you.

Adult Supervision for Children

Knot tying is a great skill for children to learn. Children always require adult supervision when working with a rope or line to ensure safety. Accidents can happen easily, so always watch children while tying knots. Help them with more difficult concepts. Do not let children independently use knives, scissors, or other dangerous objects.

Remove Potentially Hazardous Objects

Some items are a hazard while working with ropes. Jewelry, like watches or bracelets, can sustain damage when handling ropes. Long hair might get caught in a knot, and sudden movements could pull it out. Ensure your hands are free and tie your hair back if it is long. Some people secure their glasses with a strap to prevent them from falling off while handling the rope. Keep other distractions away too. Pack away your digital devices, such as cellphones or music players, so your full attention is on the equipment before you.

General Guidelines for Knot Tying

Practice Makes Perfect

Start your knot tying with a simple knot. Not everyone can master advanced knots quickly, and that is okay. Practice the eight basic knots, which are the basis for all others. Practice those eight knots until you can do them without looking at instructions. You are ready to learn new knots once you can make the basic knots from memory. The more you practice making knots, the easier it gets. Do not give up—try again.

Work Neatly

Knots are precise and clean, and making knots requires that your work area be clean, too. Ensure your workspace, such as a table, is tidy and has nothing that might be pushed over the edge while working on your knots. Wipe the surface to remove any dirt before you start.

Sometimes, your knot-making will happen outside. You might be on a camping trip, at the side of a river, or even just sitting on the grass to practice. It is still important to keep your area neat and clean. Remove any stones, rocks, or sharp objects that may damage your rope. If possible, lay down a tarp or other ground cover before you handle the rope and start making knots.

Handling The Rope

A rope stays usable and strong if you look after it properly. Never drag a rope, which causes scuffing, especially on abrasive surfaces. Rather, please pick up the rope and carry it where you need it. Check your rope for any damaged sections before you start making knots. A good practice is keeping a notebook and writing down the date you purchased a new rope. Please make a note every time you use that rope so that you will know when it has been used a lot. Replace the rope when it starts showing signs of damage or weakness.

Sometimes, cutting ropes are necessary. You might cut a rope because it is too long. Some people cut the rope when they finish making a practice knot to keep it in their collection. Other times, people cut a rope to remove a weak section. Wrap some tape around the area where the cut will be made. Make several repetitions of the tape to ensure the edges of the rope do not unravel after cutting.

Making Knots

The best knot for the job is usually the simplest to keep your objects secure and prevent slipping. Smaller knots frequently work better because there is less scuffing of the rope, but always consider loads and other factors when choosing a suitable knot. Do not handle the rope too much, as it causes scuffing and friction. Do your best on your first attempt, even if it takes longer to master the knot.

Cleaning Your Equipment

Clean ropes and lines are the best ones for tying knots. Always clean your equipment after using it. Wash your rope with mild soap and lukewarm water. Rinse the rope properly and then let it air dry. Do not use hot water or harsh chemicals, as it weakens the rope.

Storage

Store your knot supplies in a designated spot. Both synthetic and natural fiber ropes require dry and clean storage space. Braided and multi-strand ropes store well when coiled and placed in a storage container. Remove any kinks or knots before you store the item. Sometimes, large ropes are stored on spools or moving platforms to facilitate the transport of a rope to another location. A good option for smaller ropes is to store them in bags or crates that keep out dust, insects, and sunlight.

Properties of Knots

Proper knots have to follow certain properties and guidelines, which are the following:

1. **Security.** Knots must be secure to the point that they should hold themselves firm even if the rope breaks. They have to withstand adverse conditions, such as sailing or mountainous problems.
2. **Strength**. Knots also have to be strong. When knitting, you tend to make mechanisms close to crushing or breaking. These stresses only make the knots stronger, so you have to make sure that you use ropes made of the following fibers: rayon, bamboo, triacetate, diacetate, modal, and lyocell. They're all pictured below:

   - ✓ Rayon Rope
   - ✓ Bamboo Rope
   - ✓ Triacetate Rope
   - ✓ Diacetate Rope
   - ✓ Modal Rope
   - ✓ Lyocell Rope

3. **Sliding.** This means the knot shouldn't move relatively against the movable object (if any). When knots slide, the rope wouldn't be able to do what's expected of them—and that's not what you'd want to happen.
4. **Capsizing.** This means that you should be able to rearrange or re-style the parts of the knot utilizing pulling the ends—and when you do so, you have to make sure that the rest of the rope would not be affected.
5. Slipping. Ensure the rope can be pulled back with tension even if the knot is in place. You must be mindful of sliding, or the knot's quality will be affected.
6. Releasability. And, you have to take note that different knots take different matters to be released or untied. Ensure you know how your knot works so you can release them correctly, too!

Now that you know what knots are and how they're made, it's time to get acquainted with the different types of knots.

Components of Knots

To get you started, here are the various components of knots:

Bight. Bights are the slack, curved sections of the knots. They are also known as loops found near the ends of the rope, yarn, or string.

Bight

Loop. Loops are like bights but narrower and have two separate ends.

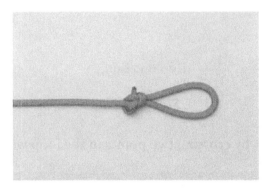

Loop

Standing End. A knot's standing end is usually the rope part that is not necessarily part of the knot.

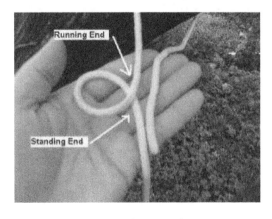

Standing End

Bitter End. Meanwhile, the knot's bitter end shows where the rope has been tied off.

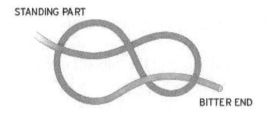

Bitter End

Standing Part. This part of the knot comes between the standing end and the knot itself.

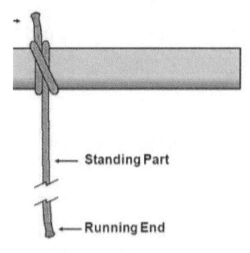

Standing Part

Elbow. You can make an elbow by crossing two points in the loop with an extra twist.

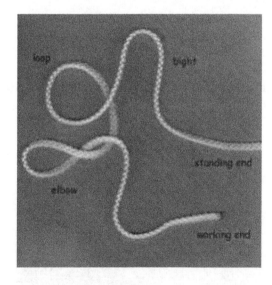

Elbow

Working Part. This is the section between the knot and the working end.

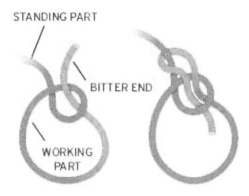

Working Part

Working End. This is the active end of the rope.

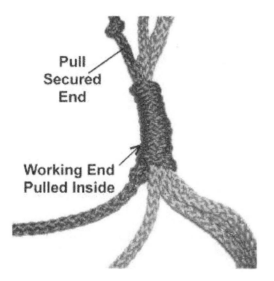

Working End

Turns. These are various types of encircling or knotting the object.

Various Turns

CHAPTER 3

BASIC KNOTS

Basic Knots are also known as the building blocks of tying. When you get to know and understand them, it will be easier to know how to make other kinds of knots featured in this book. Some of them may even look alike, and that's why they're often confused, but by learning how to make them, you definitely won't be confused anymore.

Overhand Knot

Known as the simplest of all basic and stopper knots, the Overhand Knot is mostly used to prevent the unraveling of the rope's end.

The Overhand Knot

Instructions:

1. First, make a loop and let the end pass through it.
2. Tighten the loop so you can form the overhand knot.
3. Pull it tight if you want to use it as a stopper.

Half Hitch

The Half Hitch looks like the knot has been tied with the rope's end passed through the object so you can secure it.

Instructions:

1. First, make a loop around the object.
2. Let the end pass through the loop and the standing end.
3. Tighten the loop so you can form a half-hitch. Please do it again so you can make two half-hitches.

Half Knot

The half knot is a binding knot known as the square knot's base.

Instructions:

1. Cross two ends of the rope over each other.
2. Let one pass over the end and under toward the other end. This way, the half-knot would finally be made!

Sheet Bend

Also known as the Weaver's Knot, the Sheet Bend is perfect for letting two lengths of rope come together. You could also knot them on the same side or do so on opposite sides.

Instructions:

1. First, make a bight from the thicker part of the rope, and hold it with one of your hands.
2. Let the thinner rope pass through the bight that you have made.
3. Then, let it pass through the tail or the blue rope in the example given above.
4. Let the smaller ropes pass under themselves so the knot can be finished.

The Figure is a convenient and quick stopper knot that ensures a line doesn't fall or slide out of sight—even if it comes with tight jams in the block. It's also a knot you can undo on your own, and if not done right, you'd have to retract it.

Instructions:

1. First, let the tail of the rope pass over itself so you can form a loop.
2. Then, continue the process and let it come through the loop near the standing end.
3. Complete the knot by letting the tail pass through the loop.

Slip Knot

The Slip Knot is made with the bight of the knot—by making sure it comes from the short end of the rope and not the long one. It is one of the most frequently used knots and could be used as a temporary stopper.

Instructions:

1. Form a loop near the end of the rope.
2. Then, make a bight from the short end of the rope and tuck the bight through the loop.
3. Tighten the bight, and you'd get your slip knot ready!

Noose

The Noose is almost the same as the Slip Knot, but the difference is that the bight has to be inserted from the long end of the rope. It is also one of those frequently tied knots that helps you gain control of the string. The noose is also a term given to loop knots that have tightened under load and are sometimes applied to the so-called hangman's knot.

Overhand Knot

The overhand knot is one of the most common and basic knots that most people know how to tie, and it is the foundation for countless other knots and can also work as a stopper knot.

How to tie it

- Start by forming an overhand loop
- Thread the working end upward from underneath the loop
- Pull both the standing part and the working end to tighten the knot

This knot works best when applied at the end of a rope, which helps prevent it from becoming untied when applying tension.

Advantages

- Tying it is straightforward

Disadvantages

- Depending on the type of rope used to tie this knot, if put under heavy loads, it can be very hard to untie, especially if tied using very thin cordage.

Square Knot

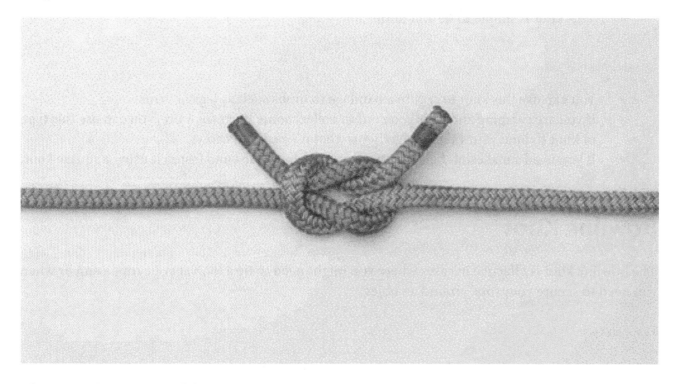

The square knot is one of the most popular, mostly used to bind objects together, and some areas of the globe call it the reef knot.

Although this knot is very popular, you should use it with a lot of caution. Most people use it to join two lengths of rope to create a longer rope, which is unsafe because square knots tend to slip or even become untied when a load is applied.

How to tie

Hold the ends of your rope in each hand. As you do this, cross the working end in your left hand over to the one in your right hand, which will result in an 'X.'

Wrap the working end you are holding in your left hand behind, then under the working end that you are holding in your right hand.

Continue wrapping the working end until it lies over the working end in your left hand—shown below.

Proceed by taking the working end in your right hand, then cross it over to the working end in your left hand to form another 'X.'

Wrap the working of the rope in your right hand behind, then under the working end in your left hand.

Continue to wrap until the working end lies over the working end in your left hand—shown below.

Now you have a standing part and working end in each of your hands. Pull them away from each other to tighten the knot.

A proper knot should have a standing part and working end over a bight. If this is not the case, you probably tied a granny knot. Below is an instance of a square knot tied improperly.

Advantages

- This knot is simple to tie and untie

Disadvantages

- You can use this knot to secure a bandage to limbs such as legs or arms.
- If you are camping and have gone out to collect some twigs for a fire, you can use this type of knot to bind your bundle together so that it's easier to carry.
- If you need a makeshift belt, tie a rope around your waist and fasten it using a square knot.

Bowline Knot

The bowline knot is effective in cases where you might need to tie a loop at your rope's end or when you need to secure your rope around an object.

How to tie

Start by forming an overhand loop on the rope's standing part.

Move the working end of the rope upward through the resulting loop from step 1

Wrap the working end of the rope behind its standing part

Continue to move the working end into and through the overhand loop you created in step 1

Complete the knot and pull it until it is tight enough

Advantages

- This knot is easy to tie and untie and fairly secure. Adding load onto a rope with this knot tends to tighten up, not become untied, which is usually the case with most other knots.
- This knot will not constrict the object you've tied around upon applying tension to the rope's standing part.

Disadvantages

- Any tension exerted on a rope with this knot makes the knot almost impossible to untie—or untying it becomes very challenging.
- Possible applications
- This knot has a wide range of applications. For instance, you can use it to secure the guy line of a tent. You can also use it to secure and tether a canoe or raft to a tree as it floats in water.

Taut Line Hitch

This knot acts as a slide that tightens or loses a loop in a line. To tie this knot, wrap the rope around a solid object like a stake to form a loop. Use the free end of the rope to wrap the mainline two times inside the loop. The next step is to lay the free end of the rope over two wraps, wrapping it around the mainline, and then drag the tag end through the loop. Then tighten the wraps by clinching them and pulling the standing line. This causes the taut-line hitch to grip the loaded line.

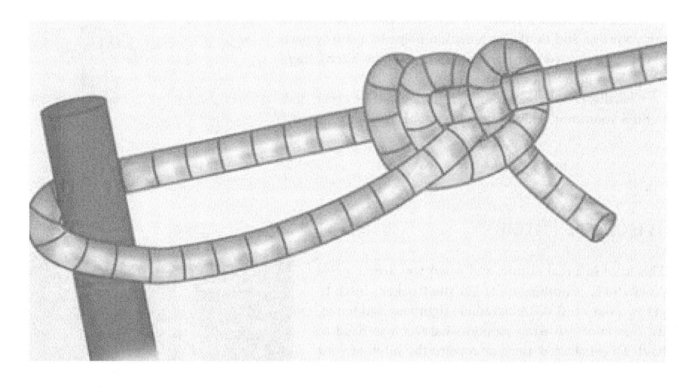

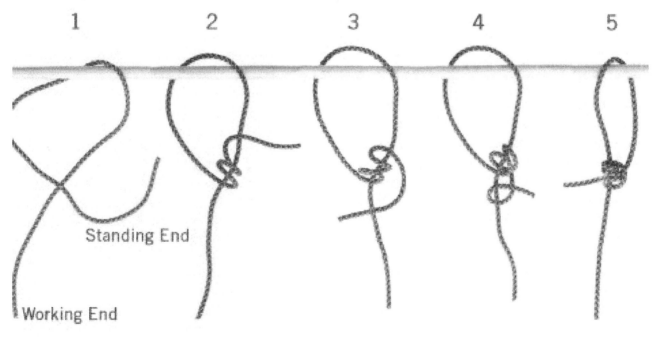

Clove Hitch Knot

This is a good knot to know if you need to secure multiple objects together quickly. In the old days, it was often used to secure things like animal-drawn carts, attaching one in a straight line. This sort of knot is also quite helpful in rock climbing. Many climbers have benefited from being able to make use of these knots in their climbing ropes.

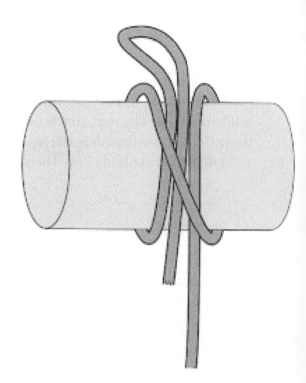

The knot itself is relatively easy to make. First, stretch out your line and tie the termination point to a sturdy part of the structure you wish to link up (this is the hitch), then wrap the rope over it multiple times.

Finally, crisscross the lines, bundle it all together, and tighten your knot. This clove hitch knot is ready to go.

Trucker's Hitch

This knot is a real classic, and when you are in a real pinch, there is nothing quite like the trucker's hitch to get you out of it! With incredible tightness and tenacity, this knot can wrap around whatever you need to haul. To get started, tie your rope to the hitch of your vehicle. Now stretch out your rope line and wrap it around whatever you are trying to haul, securing a double knot around the object. Double back the rope diagonally and tighten the string with one final knot. Your trucker's hitch is complete!

Your trucker's hitch can be used to secure hefty objects successfully. The tightness of the knots is the key to the power behind them. Feel free to tighten and loosen these knots as needed.

Timber Hitch Knot

Timber hitch knots get their name because they are created by tying them around a piece of timber or some other type of wood. For our example, you can use a sawed-off half of a piece of 2x4.

First, loop your rope around the wood and pull your rope under the loop before quickly jerking the line to the left to make your first knot. Next, double up your loop again before pulling a final knot on top.

Now give your line one more good yank to ensure it holds, and your timber hitch knot is ready for use. As you might imagine, this type of knot is ideal if you need to bundle together and carry wood piles. You can also use it well by securing your backpacks and any other luggage under one massive timber hitch knot. It is amazing how well the timber hitch knot can hold everything together.

The Rolling Hitch

To make a rolling hitch knot, you need to take a standard piece of rope and double it over at the mid-section. Next, rope one end around the other and continue wrapping the rope over each other down the entire length.

Pass the leading end underneath and tighten the rope until the knot is solid. You now have yourself a rolling hitch. This type of knot has been used by sailboats for thousands of years, and it is also worth its weight in gold when it comes to serving as special shocks for a ship's anchor.

Figure-8 Knot

Generally, this knot is utilized for sailing and rock climbing. It keeps the rope from slipping through a restraining device. The knot jams under pressure though it's easy to unfasten compared to the overhand knot that typically needs to be cut to unfasten.

The figure-8 knot is mostly used in "prusik" climbing with a locking device, proper rope, and a climbing harness. This makes it easier for the climber to descend or ascend as the knot is non-jamming.

How to Tie a Figure 8 Knot

Take a sizeable rope length and prepare it for tying the figure-8 knot:

Step 1: Create a single loop using your rope's working end.

Step 2: Bring the working end over your standing part. Create another loop by crossing the working end over your standing end.

Step 3: Slip your rope's working end into your initial loop.

Step 4: Yank either end of your rope to fasten the knot as preferred.

CHAPTER 4

CORDAGE & KNOTS

Why cord

The following section will examine the reasons for working with a cord. Because there are many options, cords, ropes, strings, and techniques such as beading, macrame, and many others, it is worth looking at paracord's benefits. That way, you can sleep at night and know you chose the right material for your crafts!

Durability

When I first read how strong paracord is, I was amazed. It can hold 550 pounds! A single cord can hold more weight than most humans weigh. Further more, a single inner strand of paracord can hold an impressive 50 pounds of weight (up to 70, actually!), and the outer wrap can hold 200 pounds by itself.

Is that not something amazing? Well, ropes and cords are amazing that way. It reminds me of the story about the strength of the spider web. That thin line made by the spider is as strong as high-grade alloy steel!

In any case, most of the things you make out of paracord are insanely durable. I don't know if anyone can rip apart a paracord with their bare hands, but a braided or knotted paracord is even stronger! People even tow their cars with braided paracord!

Price

Paracord is cheap. Considering a price of 10$ per 100 feet of cord, which is overdoing it quite a bit, you can get about a foot per 10 cents of a cord! That, my sir, is cheap. The other commonly used supplies, such as bracelet buckles, are also common, cheap, and easy to find.

The way to buy paracord is to get a good mix of colors and lengths. Having colors to select from will keep your projects from looking too boring.

Starting, you may consider getting prepackaged cords of different colors. If you plan on jumping into paracord crafts, spools of 300 or more feet are available with bulk pricing, saving you a lot of money in the long run.

A notable person in the paracord crafts once said: "You may just go ahead and buy that 300 feet spool of black paracord; you will end up using as much in the long run."

Popularity

Paracord is hot! I may be biased since I have published a book on the subject. Still, if you look at social media such as Pinterest, various Facebook groups, and websites popping up, you can easily get an idea about the size of the community.

Paracord projects are posted daily on these channels and provide a steady stream of new ideas. I must comment that a part of why I chose to write this book is because THERE ARE TOO MANY BRACELET DESIGNS OUT THERE, and that makes your life hard since you can not focus on crafting beautiful bracelets but on trying to decide on a design. This book will challenge you but also provide variety, which is of value, in my opinion.

Fun

Paracord is fun to work with. Not just because you can make some amazing things to show off to your friends. I have seen people make paracord weapons like flails, toys for kids, and even swimwear (a paracord bikini).

Because paracord crafts are so popular, making new things is always good to keep things fresh. I hope this book will help you master the paracord bracelets ad allow you to join the paracord community!

It is also a great craft to get yourself and your family into. Just imagine how your kids can grow their skills by creating things themselves.

Creativity

Paracord comes in many colors, and the patterns you can try are beyond count. Because of that, I consider knotting and working with paracord very creative. Making something new to share with your friends, family, and the world is priceless. And this book will show you how to impress your friends with various designs chosen for their traits.

The Supplies You Will Need

Paracord is a great material to work with, but there is a certain amount of supplies that you will need to get started. This chapter will list the items you need to make your paracord projects a reality. You won't find expensive or hard-to-find items in this chapter—everything presented here can be easily found at your local shopping centers.

Clipboard

A clipboard as your work space? Yes, as it turns out, a simple clipboard is a vital part of any paracord project. It helps to keep your work steady and on an even keel.

Just use a standard clipboard, so your paracord project stays on track. In truth, just about every good paracord project has a good clipboard behind it. Clipboards can be purchased at just about any office supply or department store. The sooner you get a hold of one, the sooner you can get started.

Crochet Needles

Crochet needles are a great asset for any paracord project since they make threading your paracord an absolute breeze. It's no trouble making knots and putting your paracord assemblies together if your crochet needles are on hand. Crochet needles help you care for loose ends as you bring the whole assembly together. Crochet needles can be easily found online and at most hobby stores.

Lighter

The lighter is a necessary—but often overlooked—component of working with paracord. Lighters are useful for melting the ends of the paracord together so that you can seal up knots and ensure your assembly stays in place. The lighter is used to melt and bond separate cords together. As another proof of just how versatile the paracord is, these crafty little cords are super strong yet can be melted and forged into new lengths simply with the flick of a lighter! It doesn't get any easier than that, folks!

Pair of Pliers

Pliers are a good tool to have on hand to grip your paracord fabric as you work your material properly. Your pliers need a good grip so you can easily grab hold of your material and bring it together as it ought to be.

Dura last, for example, is an excellent brand of pliers that suits this very purpose quite nicely. As the name might imply, they are meant to "last" and most certainly serve their purpose well when gripping and pulling paracord.

Scissors

Scissors are, of course, necessary to cut adequate lengths of your paracord. The best scissors to use are the standard big-handled variety. This type of scissors is ubiquitous and can be found and purchased anywhere. When cutting with them, it is best to cut in a downward motion, so you don't fray the cord. Make sure to have a pair on hand.

Tape Measurer

Some paracord enthusiasts like to use rulers or other fancy gadgets, but I've found that tape measurers work best. You can retract and extend tape measurers as much as necessary, and they most certainly save on space! They also provide a very accurate measurement. You can get a standard tape measurer at any local hardware or department store.

Adjustable Buckles

An adjustable buckle is great for a wide variety of paracord applications. If you are making a wristband watch or a utility belt to put around your waste, you will need some form of the adjustable buckle to snap it all in place. These buckles are commonly made with metal, plastic, or even fiberglass. Each type has its strengths and weaknesses, and it's up to you to decide which would work best for your current project. All items in this chapter should go to the top of your list the next time you go on a supply run!

Cords

Some cords have an outer covering called a mantle, like Military 550 (parachute). This woven sheath protects inner strands or cords and is often made of polymer material. Seven strands are contained within the mantle in the actual 550 cables. Most survival-type manuals refer to the 550 cord because many of the older survival manuals were mostly based on military theories, and the military had plenty of 550 cords. As a result, the 550 cord is well-liked in the camping community. Ropes and cords were traditionally made of natural materials like hemp, cotton, jute, or sisal.

You can utilize a variety of cord types in the wilderness. However, I believe the mariner's tarred twisted nylon twine is the best cordage on the market. It is constructed from three synthetic fibers that are braided together. It is available in thin diameter, practical packages, with line test strengths ranging from roughly 80# test to over 500# test (these numbers relate to the twine's tensile strength). The classic para cord's (550) major flaw is that it can only be used in its unaltered state. The seven core strands tend to fray and split apart once the mantle is removed. Due to this, increasing the length of your cordage by cutting it into smaller pieces or reducing its diameter is challenging. Lillian builds cane poles, while Para cord creates improvised fishing lures. However, when used for lashings or bindings, tarred mariner's line bonds effectively to itself, breaks down readily into three smaller strands, and has a tar coating that protects it from UV radiation. I typically carry a 1# roll of the #12 and #36 sizes. The #12 works well for fishing and creating nets, while the #36 is suitable for any heavier lashings and bindings or for adding tarp guy lines.

Rope

I prefer my rope to be made of a natural substance like hemp instead of a cord. The primary cause is that it is flammable, which makes it easier to start fires and build bird nests (discussed later). Ropes can be used for various purposes, including straps for bedrolls and improvised packs. It can be used as a belt for your outermost clothing so that you don't have to dig around under your coat or blanket shirt for your sheath knife and belt pouch. Additionally, a rope can be used for various camp duties, including hanging a hammock, pulling tent stakes, dangling game animals for processing, and creating a makeshift windlass to move large objects. When tramping alone, I advise carrying around two ropes 12 feet long and one rope 25 feet long at all times.

Webbing

Because climbing uses tubular webbing, which has a high tensile strength to guard against breaking, compared to a rope, it is better because it is lighter, takes up less space, and has a higher tensile strength. When you create improvised straps from this material, you'll discover it is significantly more comfortable across distance than rope. Webbing is flat so that it may be carried in greater quantities. I advise using two 20' sections of webbing and if space and weight permit, a 50' section, as webbing generally take up less space than rope. Except for aiding in starting a fire, this material can accomplish anything rope can—and in most circumstances, a little better. You can always keep both in your bag, as I do.

Mule Tape

Electricians use mule tape, a mantle without interior strands. You can carry 100' of it without adding more than a few pounds to your bag because of its extremely high tensile strength compared to its size. I respect the strong belief in this product by Canadian author and Boreal bushcraft instructor Mors Kochanski. The atmosphere is crucial, just like all the other kit components. Mantle-type cord or rope is impractical in the eastern woodlands due to the abundance of briars, cat claws, and thorns in general and the breaking of the fibers and weaves over time. However, it is wonderful for everything a heavier rope can do if your environment permits it.

Making Natural Cordage

To create a natural cord, you must first know the appropriate material. Depending on its use, it must be reasonably powerful and accessible throughout the four seasons. The eastern woodlands contain a variety of plants and trees that naturally form cords. You only need to look as far as vines or the ground-level roots of spruce trees to find enough natural material to produce one string of adequate strength. Before a need occurs, it is best to test local materials by harvesting a section and attempting to make an overhand knot in the rope. Some of these can be rather strong. Making three or four wraps around your finger without splitting or breaking might be acceptable for some jobs, but if doing so breaks the cord, it might not be practical for some chores.

Reverse-Wrap Two-Ply Cordage

The inner barks of the tulip tree or the shagbark hickory will make the ideal material for this type of string in the eastern woodland (yellow poplar). Yucca, nettle, and dogbane are alternatives for plant fibers outside the eastern woods. The simplest and strongest string to create is from yellow poplar, which may be made in any required diameter. The least acceptable cordage material is dead or recently fallen poplar, but it will be the easiest to gather. Depending on the branch or tree, pry the bark's edge with a knife and peel it off; it should come off in large strips. To access the inner bark fibers, first, remove the outer bark. Work the piece around a rough-barked sapling or a rope to do this; this will cause the outer bark to become loose and fall off. The fibers must first be further processed into smaller strands and then into groups of strands to get the appropriate cord diameter.

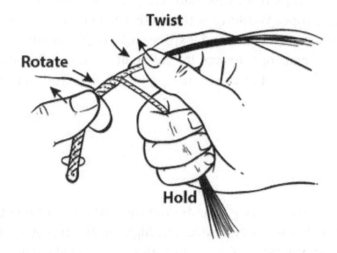

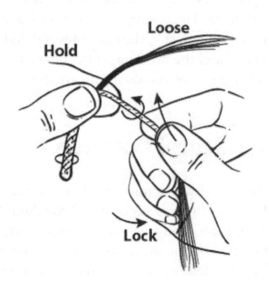

How to make cordage

Separate the strands into two bundles when you're ready to start. Twist each bundle one at a time in the same direction while holding both simultaneously but keeping them apart. To finish, pinch both bundles together and twist them in the opposite direction (i.e., they are reverse wrapped and twisted first one way and then against themselves the other time). It is best to start with bundles two different lengths apart to add length to the cable. Never do this concurrently; always only one side at a time. Add another bundle on that side, twisting it with the tail to make it one bundle when you are about 1" from the end of the shortest bundle. Once the splice is within the cord, continue wrapping in reverse as usual. You can always utilize two fully processed cords and link them together using the same technique if a stronger cord is necessary. If you do this, you will get about two-thirds of the initial strength of a single strand with the same diameter. To make a stronger cable, employ this method with cords like mariner's tarred twisted nylon twine.

Knots

Stop Knot

A stop knot is a straightforward overhand knot tied at the end of a line to prevent the rope from slipping. The knot functions as a security measure well with any other

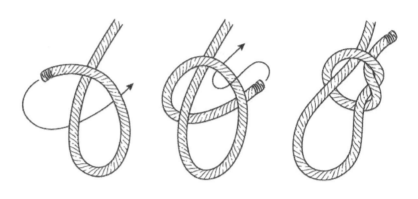

knot. Typically, you want this straightforward overhand knot to have some tail that extends past the knot. To ensure that a line or knot won't come undone if a knot does slip, tie a simple overhand stop knot on the tag end. The stop knot will prevent the line from passing through entirely.

Slipknot

Bowline Knot

One of the four fundamental mariner knots is the bowline knot, pronounced BO-lin. This knot serves as both a stand-alone and standard knot in rescue operations. This knot is perfect for attaching a static loop to the end of any line since it keeps two-thirds of the line's tensile strength even when loaded. The only drawback to this

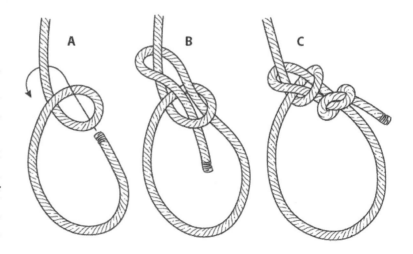

knot is that, depending on the type of cord used to make it, it has the propensity to slip or come undone when carrying a big load. However, a stop knot on the tail makes it simple to get around this.

Bowline knot

The bowline knot is best for any end-of-the-line application where you need a loop to pass the line through and tighten around an object, such as the ridgeline of a shelter. This knot will be easy enough to remove even if great stress is placed on the line. It is useful for incorporating other knots, such as the lark's head, tarp tie-out lines, and toggles at the end of a line.

Lark's Head Knot

This self-tightening knot can be tied in some ways, such as to attach toggles with a stop knot or to join two lines together to hang something from a toggle. The lark's head knot is composed of two basic loops. However, if this knot is forced to move side to side under a particularly large load, it will slip (unlike the prusik knot). When utilizing two ropes of differing diameters, with the lark's head being the smaller cord, it works especially well for tarp adjustment lines. This is the second-most adaptable knot for use in the woods, in my opinion.

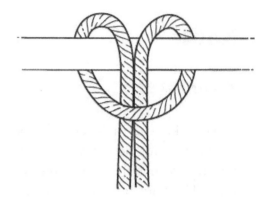

Lark's Head Knot

Jam Knot

The jam knot is a slip knot that, when used with a stop knot, jams a loop of line to tighten around an object. This knot is easily released by pulling the tail on the stop knot portion of the line. This is one of the most useful knots for its adaptability.

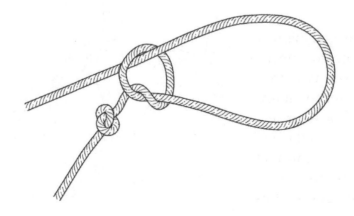

Jam knot

Trucker's Hitch

A combination of two slip knots, this knot is used for putting a line under tension and keeping it taut. It can be used for any application when a line must be drawn tight, but it will still easily be released for adjustment or recovery.

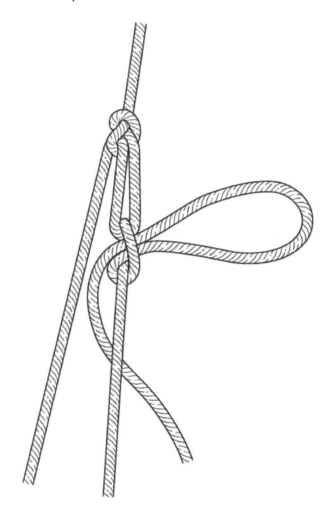

CHAPTER 5

USEFUL KNOTS

Fisherman's Knot

As the name implies, this knot is useful with a fishing line. To tie this knot, pass the free end of your line through the object (an example is through the eye of a fishhook). Wrap the free end of the line around the other part of your line four times. The next step is to pass the line's free end through a triangular opening next to the secured object. Pass the free end of your line through the large loop by going in through the small triangle. Ensure you lubricate before tightening the knot to avoid getting damaged due to heat from friction.

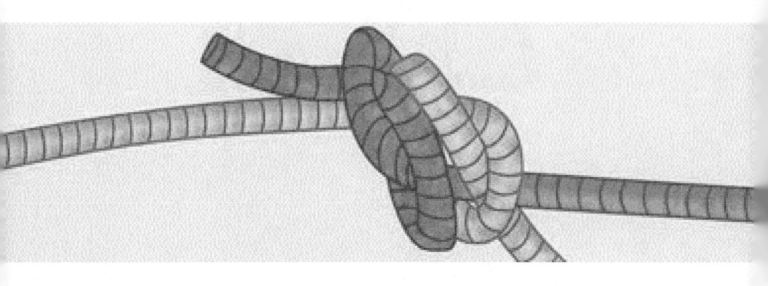

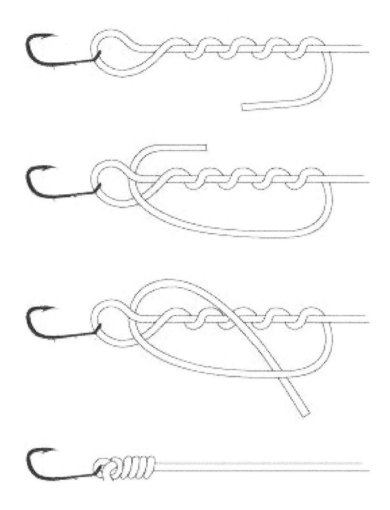

Water Knot

 The water knot secures webbings, belts, and also most straps. To tie a water belt knot, make a loose overhand knot at one end of the strap, then pass the other strap in the opposite direction. Take both ends of the strap and pull to tighten the knot.

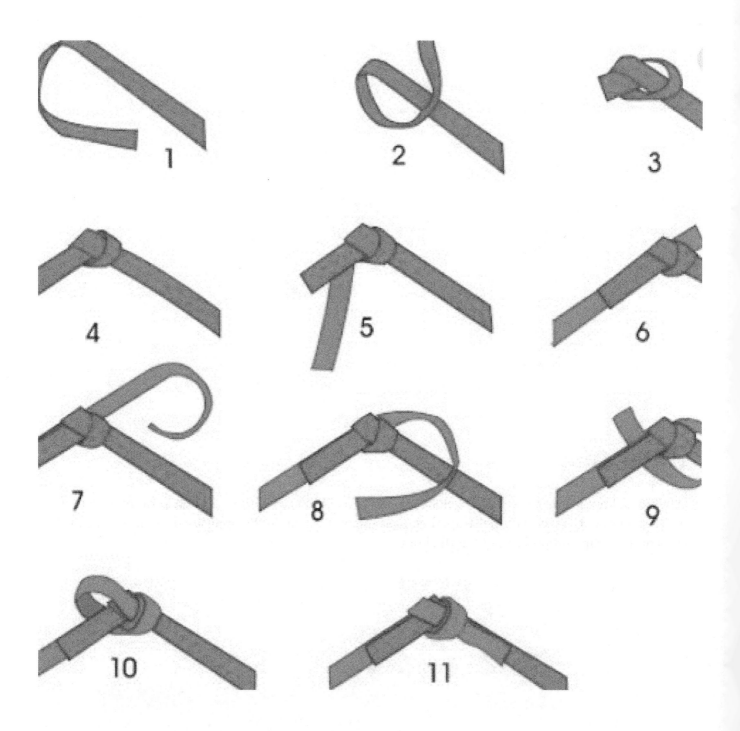

Rolling Hitch

The Rolling Hitch can be added to any existing line and hook dogs to a dog sled line. To tie this knot, wrap one end of the rope around the main rope, thus creating a Half hitch. Create another hitch (half) and wrap over the entire knot to finish with the last hitch, which is to the other side from where you started.

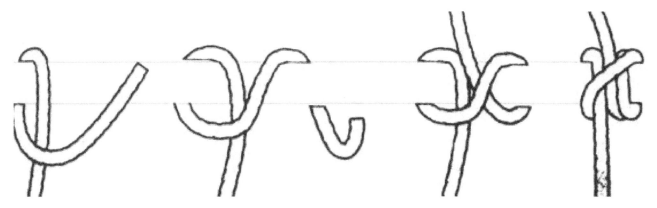

Prusik Knot

This knot is a slide and grip knot that can add a loop to a rope if both ends are not free. This knot creates a loop that can be used as an ascender or a descender. To tie this knot, you need two ropes, a short rope and a long one. The first step is to tie a loop in the short rope, which is secured with a Square knot, then wrap the loop three times around the long rope, ensuring each wrap is flat against the long rope. Now you should pass the loop of the short rope under itself and pull it to make it tight.

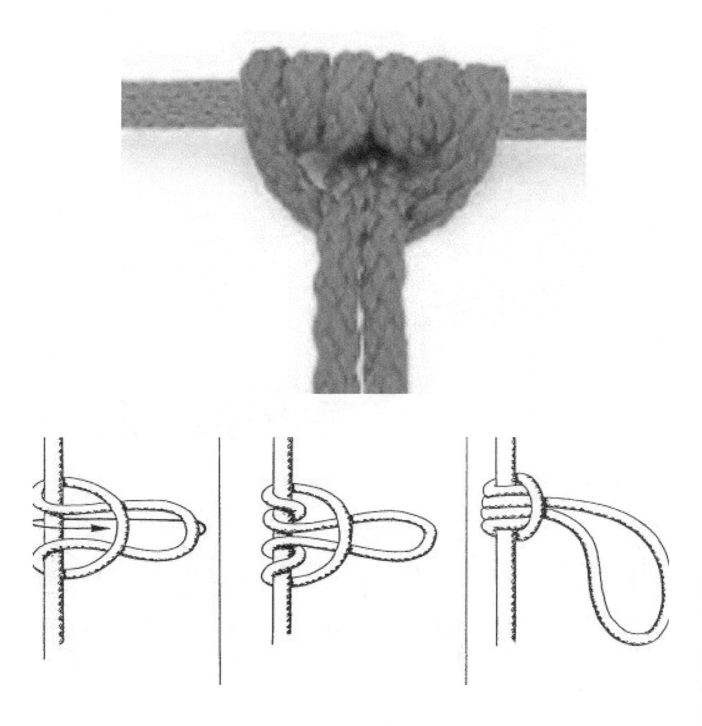

Timber Hitch

The timber hitch can be tied around rough cylindrical objects such as poles, posts, and logs. To tie a timber hitch, run the free end of the rope around the object of interest, then wrap the rope's tag end around the inside of the loop five times. Then you tighten to ensure the wraps hold firmly on the object. The timber hitch is easy to untie when you are done.

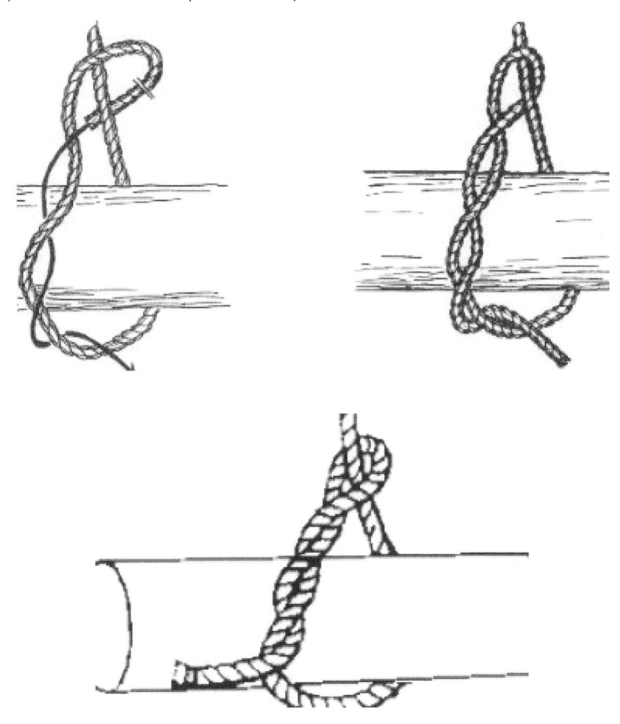

Blood Knot

This knot is used on a fishing line to join two lines together. To tie this knot, overlap both lines, wrapping the free end around the end of the other line around five times. Then pass the free end between both lines, wrap the other line five times, and tuck the free end between both lines in the opposite direction of the free end of the line.

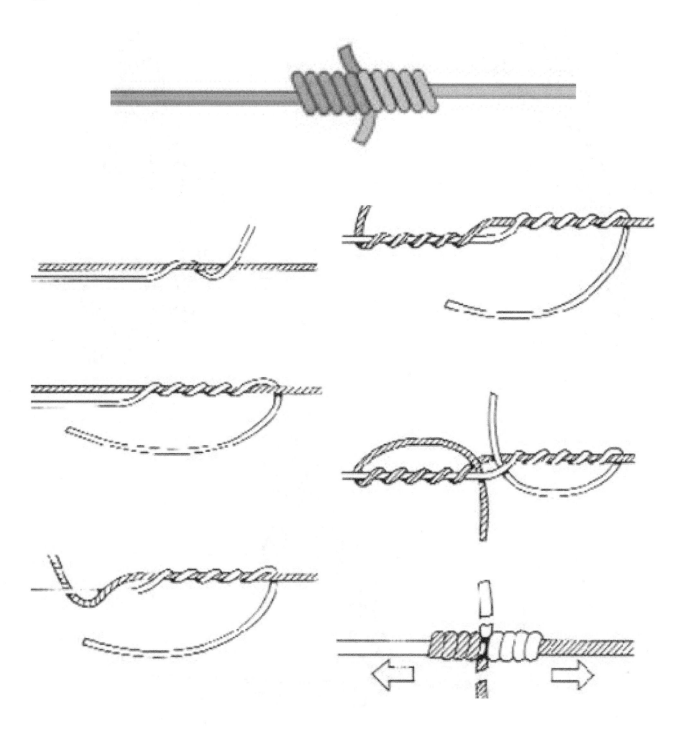

Main Harness

This knot can be used in many ways by creating strong loops. To tie this knot, create some slack in the line and make a loop so that part of the line runs through its middle(i.e., through the middle of the loop). Take the side of the loop and pull it through the gap between the line in its middle and the other side of the loop. The next step is to pull the loop tight and pull the line, thus cinching the knot. Ensure you keep something in the loop to hold it to prevent it from slipping off.

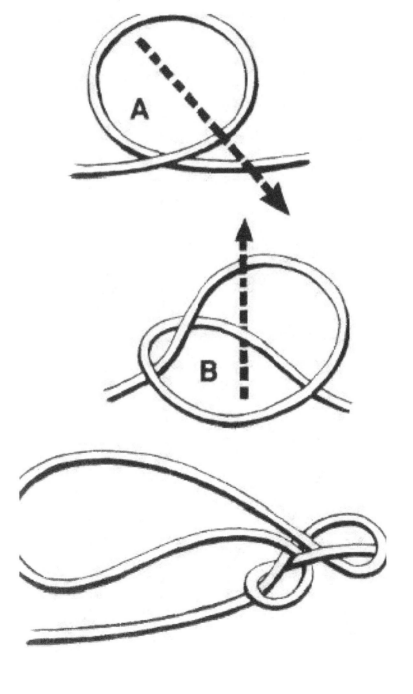

Carrick Bend

This is a knot that can be used to join two ropes together. To tie this knot, form a loop from the free ends of one rope, then pass the free end of the other rope under the first loop, then over the loop. The next step is to thread the free end across the loop by passing it under itself and finally pulling both ends to tighten the knot.

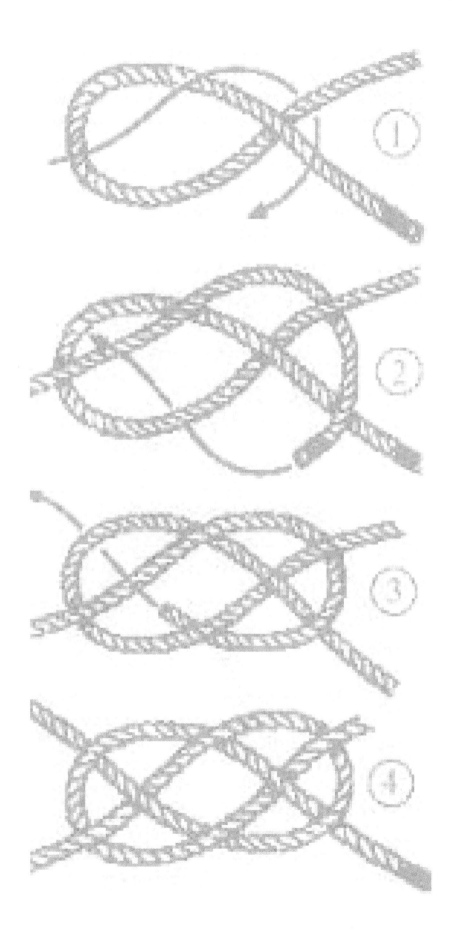

Trucker's Hitch

This hitch gives you a mechanical advantage when tightening a line. To tie this knot, tie a figure 8 knot with a loop, pass the free end of the line through what you are attaching the rope to, pass the line through the loop and pull the working end very tight, and then secure the free end with two half hitches.

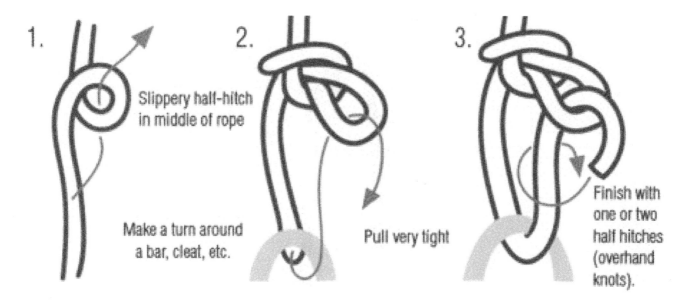

1.

Slippery half-hitch
in middle of rope

Make a turn around
a bar, cleat, etc.

2.

Pull very tight

3.

Finish with
one or two
half hitches
(overhand
knots).

Barrel Hitch

The barrel hitch knot can be used in sailing and construction to carry items like buckets, barrels, or other cylindrical objects. To tie this knot, put your object of interest on top of the rope and then tie an overhand knot across the top of the object. The next step is to open the overhand knot till it wraps around the top sides of the object. Then you tie both ends of the rope with a square knot and lift.

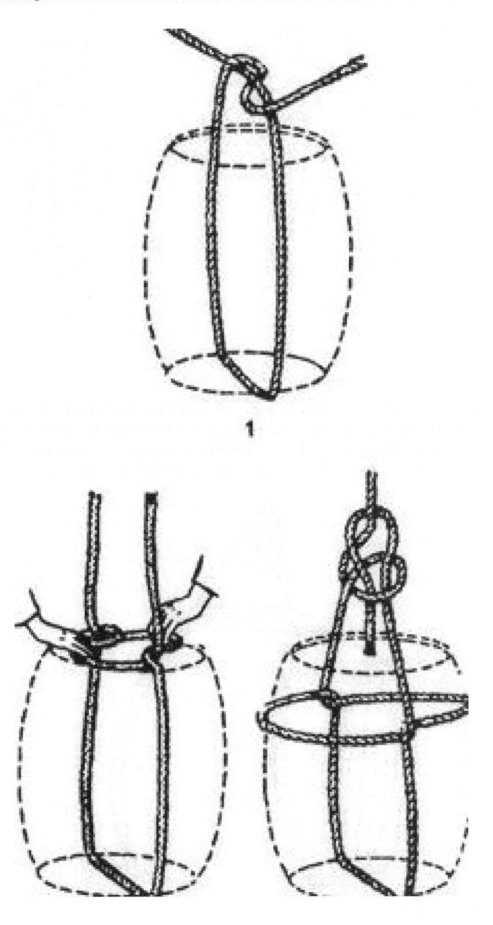

1

Sheepshank

To tie the sheepshank knot, fold the rope to the length you want, then create a half hitch with one end of the continuing rope and place it over the nearby loop. The next step is to make a half hitch at the other standing end, then drop it over the adjacent loop and tighten everything.

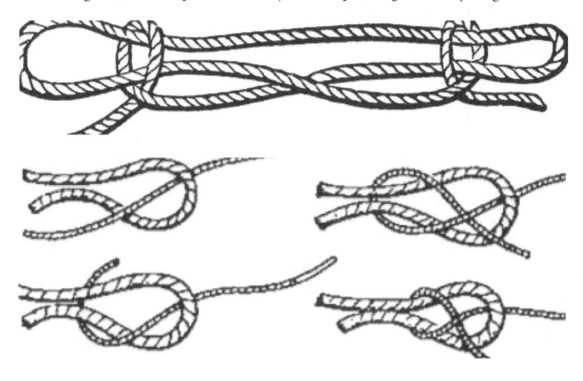

Tripod Lashing

The tripod-lashing knot can create water filters and shelters and support other things used in camps. To tie this knot, start by collecting three poles (Tripod) of similar length and thickness, lay them on the ground, tie a clove hitch to one of the poles, and then wrap around all poles five times. The next step is to wrap the line between the poles two times, working backward to the first hitch. Tie the tag end of the line to the tag end of the first knot and spread the legs of the poles.

 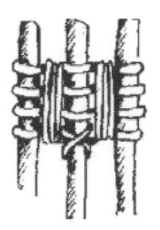 

Square Lashing

The Square Lashing is the last knot on our list. It can be used in camp chairs, bridges, and other things, and securing poles together. To tie this knot, tie a clove hitch to one of the poles you intend to use, wrap the line around where both poles meet, and ensure it goes under the lower pole and over the top pole. Then you spiral with outward wraps six times, then make a wrap between the poles, thus tightening the previous wraps. The last step is to use a square knot to tie the free end of the rope to the free end of the clove hitch.

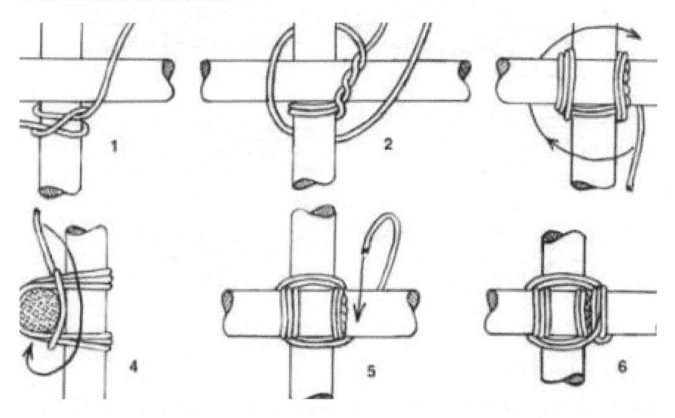

CONCLUSION

Knot tying is an effortless mechanical skill that will always be familiar if you repeatedly practice making the skills natural. When you face stressful circumstances, you will need the skill to kick in naturally so that your muscles and hands can work automatically without much thought.

Just think about when you learned to tie your shoes or lash your books together to make them easier to haul around; you probably don't even recall when it happened, but every time you need to carry out those activities, the skill comes out naturally.

So, practice, practice, practice; It's the only way to go!

At first glance, knot-making may seem like one of those strange niche hobbies that only people with a lot of time on their hands would be interested in. But this couldn't be farther from the truth. Knot-making is a vital skill that could save your life in a true survival situation.

If you were stuck out in the wilderness and needed to get safely from one ledge to another, a well-knotted rope could be the best thing in your arsenal. Also, if you need to lug up some heavy items, a knot such as a barrel knot will give you that capability. In short, if you ever find yourself in a precarious situation, you might find nothing like a good knot!

BOOK 2

The Everyday Knots Guide

INTRODUCTION

In our busy world, we tend to look for ways to have some hobbies to release some of the stress that we are experiencing. Some overlook this important part because we are busy chasing our dreams and aspirations. We forget to do something to release the stress accumulated from the stressful things we do, particularly in our work.

There are various reasons why people tend to skip hobbies, such as finances, the avoidance of learning something new, and many more. Regarding personal experience, I was also like that before, and I do not have any hobbies because I am lazy to learn something new.

Thankfully, a friend introduced me to this hobby called "knot tying," I never thought I would get hooked to this kind of hobby because at first, I thought it was boring as you are just sitting tying ropes.

But I was wrong because this hobby is really enjoyable as you can create different patterns of knots that will make you feel satisfied and your experience memorable. Since I learned knot tying, all my stress has been reduced, especially when I am doing this knot tying after work.

Let us not delay your learning, and let us start doing the projects!

CHAPTER 1

EVERYDAY KNOTS

Knots For Shoes

NOTE: In this chapter, we refer to the yellow lace o as the left lace and the blue lace as the right shoelace—from the perspective of the person wearing the shoe.

The Starting Knot

Almost all shoelace knots use the left-over-right starting knot, also called the 'overhand knot' or 'a a half knot.' This knot is the base for all knots discussed in this chapter:

How to tie

Hold one lace in your right hand and the other in your left. Cross the left lace's working end over the right shoelace's working end to form a crossing point.

Wrap the tight working end around the front of the left working end, which will end at the back of the gap between the two laces.

Pass the right lace through the gap between the two laces until it reaches the front right-hand side.

Now pull both ends to complete and tighten the knot.

The Standard Shoelace Knot

Also referred to as the loop, swoop and pull, or the Bunny Rabbit knot, this is one of the most used knots to tie shoes.

How to tie

Begin with a starting knot—explained earlier.

Now form the right working end into a bight—as shown below.

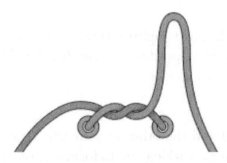

Pass the left working end behind the right loop.

Create a wrap around the right loop with the left lace so that it ends up in front.

Now push the left lace into the hole between the two laces—as shown below.

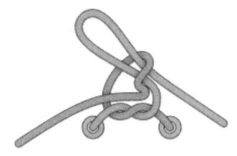

Pull the left lace from the side until it comes out to form another loop. Now you have two loose loops.

Then grab both the right and left loops and pull them to tighten and complete the knot

Double Shoelace Knot

The double shoelace knot, also called the shoe clerk's knot, is a crude way of making a knot consume excess lace to prevent the ends from dragging, which makes it quite bulky

How to tie

Begin by making the standard shoelace knot as described earlier. Make your loops long enough to work within the next steps.

Now cross the left loop over the front of your right loop, as shown below

Wrap the right loop around the back of the left loop, then feed its end into the gap between the two laces

You have just formed another overhand knot on top of the first one. Pull the two ends of the loops to tighten your knot.

Boat Shoe Knot

Also called the heaving line knot, Eastland knot, or barrel tassel, this knot is common on deck shoes—boat shoes—or moccasins with leather laces. Instead of the usual knots, it creates decorative coils and works by coiling each end of the lace around itself until there's no more lace.

How to tie

Unlike all the other shoe-related knots, this knot does not start with the starting knot.

On the contrary, you start by forming one end of your lace into a loop by doubling it back onto itself. However, you should ensure that you leave a long enough working end, and you will have a better idea of the length to leave as you continue practicing.

You should note that making this loop too long will make the working end too short and unable to complete all the wraps required to cover the loop. On the other hand, if the loop is too short, you won't have enough room to spend the excess lace. You will have a tiny coil and a long working end protruding from the top of your knot.

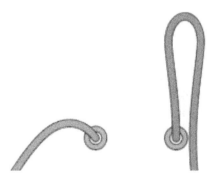

Wrap the end of your shoelace once around the lower part of the loop you formed. In this case, the direction of the wrap does not matter, and you can wrap it either way—around the back or the front.

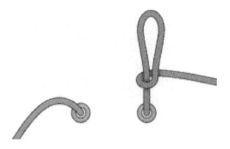

Wrap the end of the shoelace again around the loop immediately above the first one you made

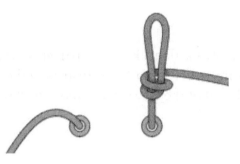

Continue to wind the end of your lace around the loop until it gets to the top. As you do this, ensure you make it as tight as possible around the loop and as snuggly as possible against previous loops, resulting in a tight lace coil.

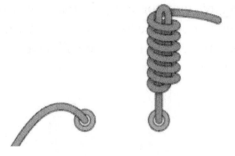

Feed the end of your shoelace through the remaining top of your loop. You can now pull the whole coil upwards, and that will pinch the top of your loop tightly to secure the loose end.

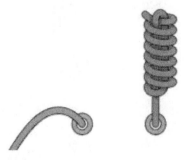

Repeat all the above steps with the other lace to end up with two separate coils—as shown below.

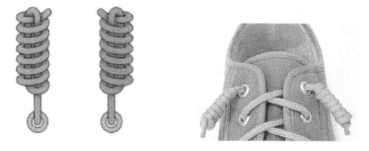

Eye Splice

How to tie it:

Decide how far back on the rope you will use, and secure this in place. You can use glue or tape or keep an eye on it to ensure you do not unwind more than you intend to as you unwind the rope.

Unravel enough of the rope back toward this point to make 5 passes on the main body of the rope.

Once you have this amount ready, you will take one of the strands and pass it under one of the standing strands on the main frame of your rope. Pass the next rope in line under the lower standing strand on the rope.

You will now have the upper strand that you must pass under the upper standing strand on your rope.

Go back to the beginning now, and take another one of the strands and pass it under one of the standing strands on the main frame of your rope. Pass the next rope in line under the lower standing strand on the rope.

You will now have the upper strand that you must pass under the upper standing strand on your rope.

Go back to the beginning now, and take another one of the strands and pass it under one of the standing strands on the main frame of your rope. Pass the next rope in line under the lower standing strand on the rope.

You will now have the upper strand that you must pass under the upper standing strand on your rope.

Continue this process until you have run out of the open rope you were using. Pull tightly, or burn the rope to hold it against itself, and you are done.

Granny Knot

How to tie it:

You will use 2 lengths of rope to create this knot or 1 long length of rope that has been folded over itself.

Start with the ends of the ropes, and loop one end over the other, going from left to right.

Make sure you leave plenty of room at the ends of the rope when you complete this first pass.

You are now going to take the 2 ends you have just looped over each other and turn them back against each other. This time, you will loop them through each other again, going from left to right again.

Now use both hands to pull on all 4 ends of the rope you have in place. This will secure the knot against itself, sealing it in place.

Double Bow Line

How to tie it:

This knot requires a lot of rope, so ensure you have enough to work with before you begin. If you ever need a knot without enough rope, default to the normal bowline.

Using the rope's end, you will make a loop, then follow this loop with another loop. You are going to now overlap the two loops against each other. Wrap one of the loops around the main body of the rope, then push it through the first loop you have made on the rope.

You will slide the end of this loop up and over the loop you have just created, then pull it tight to secure the knot in place.

Nail Knot

How to tie it:

You will need 2 lines of rope for this or a main piece (such as a nail) and another length of rope. To create this knot, you will lay both ropes against each other, preferably with something such as a nail between them.

Please take one of the ropes and pass it over and around the main line of the other rope and the nail. You will now wrap this in place several times (at least 6) around the nail and the other rope.

Pull out the nail from the center now, and gently slide the end of the rope you have just used to wrap this in place through the center of the loops. This will take some patience, and it may work best if you use some lubricant to slide it through the main part of the rope.

Once you have worked this line through the rope, pull it tightly on both ends, and secure it in place.

Diamond (Lanyard) Knot

It is also referred to as the knife lanyard knot, Bosun's Whistle knot, or the friendship knot. We use the diamond knot to form a decorative, fixed loop at the center of a rope or small cord (such as a paracord). You may also use leather and lanyards to make this knot.

How to Tie a Diamond Knot

Step 1: Start by forming a loop, then circle the rope around it.

Step 2: Slip a section of your rope across the loop you just created.

Step 3: Lead that end upward, then cross it through the initial loop.

Step 4: Hold the bigger loop, then tighten the knot by yanking the ends.

CHAPTER 2

HOUSEHOLD KNOTS

Sheet Bend Knot

Also called a weavers knot, this knot is ideal in cases where you have to join two ropes with different diameters. However, it's not limited to ropes with varying diameters; you can also use it to join ropes with similar diameters.

How to tie

Start by making a bight on the rope's working end with a thicker diameter. Hold it in your right hand.

Keep the 'U' of the bight facing the right and the ropes working at the bight's top.
Then take the rope with the thinner diameter and thread it upwards from the bottom of the bight you formed in step 1

Now move the working of the thin rope around and behind the bight of the other rope. It is essential to wrap it in such a way that it goes towards the direction the working end of the thick rope is facing

Thread the working end of the rope with the smaller diameter under itself—shown in the image below

Dress and then finally tighten your knot

Advantages

Even though tying knots using ropes of different diameters can cause the knot to become unstable and prone to slipping, this knot can solve this issue.

Disadvantages

This knot tends to get loose when you apply tension on both ropes

Possible applications

If you need a longer rope, and all you have is the option of using different types of scavenged rope, all of which have different diameters, then this knot will come in handy.

Double Sheet Bend

The double sheet bend is slightly modified to the sheet bend knot but is purposed to become more secure.

How to tie

Form a bight using the rope's working end with the thick diameter and hold it in your left hand.

Keep the 'U' of the bight facing the right; you should position the working end at the top.

Hold the thinner rope in your right hand and thread it upwards from the bottom of the bight.

Move the working end of the thin rope around and behind the bight. Wrap it towards the direction the bight's working end faces (shown in the above steps).

Thread the working end of the thin rope under itself, then create a second wrap by repeating steps 4 and 5.

Finish by tightening and dressing the knot. You will end up with a knot that looks like the one in the image below:

Possible applications

You can use this knot anywhere where you would need to use a sheet bend knot and in situations where you need a more secure knot

The Double Fisherman's Knot

In some situations, you may need to tie together two lengths of rope to make a longer one. This knot, in some cases referred to as the 'grapevine knot,' is what you should use in such circumstances.

This knot is a constituent of two knots that lock onto each other when you apply tension to the rope.

How to tie

Start by Laying the working ends of each of the ropes parallel to one another. Let the ends overlap by a few inches—shown in the image below. The rope diameter you use will determine how much overlap you need. Thin ropes such as paracord will require a little overlap compared to thicker ropes that may need more overlap. As you continue to practice with this knot, you will be able to develop a sense of how much overlap you should leave.

Cross the working end of your rope over to the other rope standing part and wrap it behind it. Then move around it to the top—shown in the image below.

Form another wrap, ensuring you keep it on the left side of the crossing point of the previous wrap—shown below.

Thread your working end through the two wraps you formed—moving the rope below the crossing points on the two wraps.

Dress the knot and pull to tighten it. At this stage, you have completed the first part of the knot, and the next part involves repeating the whole process on the other length of rope.

Cross the rope's working end to the other rope's standing part. When you complete this step, you should end with the working end facing downward—shown in the image below.

Create another wrap, keeping it at the right side of the crossing point you formed in step 6.

Thread the working end under the crossing points of both the wraps you created. Dress the knot and pull to tighten it. You have completed the second part of the knot, which should look like the image below.

Pull on each of the standing parts of the two ropes to complete the knot. The knots will slide together, and you will end up with a knot like the one shown below.

Square Knot

The first on our list is the square knot. This knot is useful for connecting ropes and lines and joining cut ropes back together. To tie a square knot, lap one rope right over the left, followed by passing it underneath the other. And then tying it again in the opposite direction, i.e., left over right, and then passing it underneath. If you do this well, each rope's working and standing ends will be side by side.

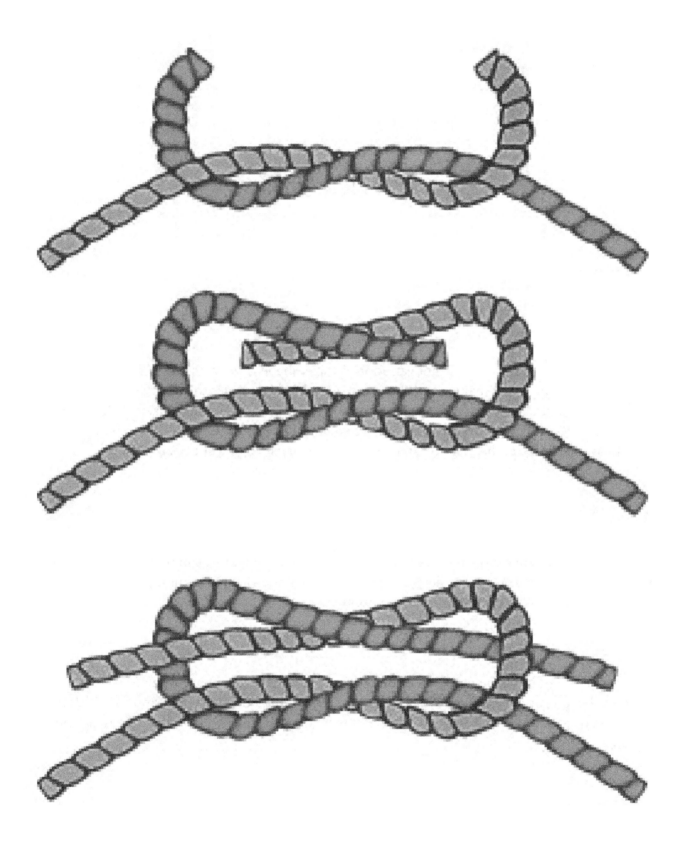

CHAPTER 3

NECKTIES KNOT

Necktie Knots

Knots for neckties have significant variations in size, shape, and symmetry for different knots. Therefore, when making a necktie knot, you should consider the length of the tie, the thickness of the material used to make the tie, and the desired look. Every knot has a distinct character, and thick ties usually require you to use smaller knots, while thinner ties look better with larger ones.

Below are some of the most common knots you can use to tie your tie:

The Four In Hand Knot

The four-in-hand knot is the most common necktie knot because it is simple to tie and can be ideal for most occasions. The knot is slender and slightly asymmetrical. The knot comes from the name of a gentleman's club founded in the 19th century.

How to tie

Begin with the small end of your tie on your left and the wide end on your right. Make the small end slightly above your belly button, which may vary depending on your height and the thickness and length of your tie. Note that you will only be moving the working end of the tie (the wide end).

Now pass the working end over the small end -towards the left.

Pass the working end under the small end—towards the right.

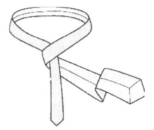

Continue moving the working end across the front and towards the left.

From underneath the neck loop, move the working end upwards.

Move it back down into the loop you made now formed in the front (loosen a little bit if necessary)

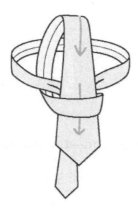

Now pull the working end downwards to tighten the knot. Slide the knot upwards to adjust.

The Eldredge Knot

This knot is eye-catching, complex, and unorthodox. Invented in 2007 by Jeffrey Eldredge, it became famous on the internet in 2008. Unlike most necktie knots, the Eldredge knot uses the small end of the tie as the working end. When completed, you tuck the excess small end behind the shirt collar.

Regarding size, this knot is large and creates a tapered fishtail braid effect. You should wear this tie cautiously as it does not suit some occasions.

How to tie

Begin with the small end of the tie on the right and the wide end on you the left. Adjust the tie, so the tip of the wide end rests at the top of your belt buckle. In this section, the working end will be the small end of your tie.

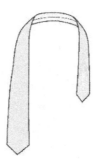

Now pass the small end to the wide end —towards the left.

Pass the small end under the wide end —towards the right.

Continue moving it towards the neck loop up to the center.

Move it into the neck loop, then towards the left.

Pass it across the front, then to the right. From underneath, Move it upwards into the neck loop.

Move it downwards to the left, then around the back of the wide end, towards the right; do not tighten this part.

Pass the small end across the front, to the left, and finally, through the loop, you created in the previous step.

Pull the small end of the tie to the left to tighten.

Continue to pass it up to the center, then towards and into the neck loop, and finally pass it to the left.

Move it upwards to the center, towards the neck loop. Pass it downwards through the neck loop and towards the right. Do not tighten this part.

Pass it across the front of the tie to the left through the loop you created in the above step.

Pull the working end to the left to tighten your knot.

Tuck the excess part of the small end behind the left side of the neck loop.

Van Wijk Knot

This necktie knot is cylindrical and incredibly tall, and its invention came from an attempt to create the tallest wearable tie knot possible by an artist called Lisa Van Wijk. When tied correctly, this knot creates an unmistakable and striking helical effect.

How to tie

Begin by placing the small end of your tie on the left and the wide end on the right. Adjust the tie so that the tip of the small end rests slightly above your belly button. That, however, may vary depending on your height and the thickness and length of your tie. The working end is the wide end of your tie.

Pass the wide end over the small end – towards the left.

Continue to pass it under the small end, then towards the right.

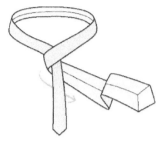

Pass it across the front of the tie, then towards the left.

Pass it under the small end, then move it towards the right.

Pass it across the front of the tie, then towards the left.

Pass it under the small end, then towards the right.

Pass it across the front of the tie again, then towards the left.

From underneath, move it upwards through the neck loop.

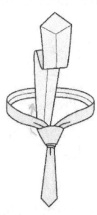

Pass it downward, then under the three loops formed before the tie (loosen if necessary).

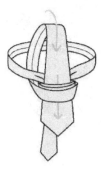

Pull down on the wide end of the tie to tighten the knot. Slide your knot upwards to adjust. It is normal for the first and second loops on the knot to show slightly under the third loop.

The Trinity Knot

Like the Eldredge knot, the trinity knot is a recent innovation that also tied using the small end as the working end and tied very loosely initially, then pulled to tighten at the end.

This knot produces a slightly asymmetrical and rounded shape, and it is visually striking and slightly larger than some common necktie knots.

How to tie

Begin by placing the small end of your tie to the right and the wide end to the left. Adjust the tie, so the tip of the wide end rests at the top of your belt buckle. For these instructions, you will only be using the small end.

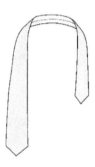

Pass the small end over the wide end, then towards the left.

From underneath, Pass it upwards into the neck loop.

Pass it downwards and towards the left.

Pass it around the back of your wide end, then towards the right.

Move it upwards to the center and then into the neck loop.

Pass it through the neck loop, then downwards towards the left.

Pass it across the front of the wide end, then upwards into the neck loop.

Pass it downwards through the loop you formed above. Do not tighten it.

Pass the small end behind the wide end —towards the right.

Bring it across the front of the wide end towards the center. Pass it through the loop you created in the step above.

Tighten your knot and tuck the excess part of the small end behind the left side of your neck loop

Bow tie Knot

At the end of the 19th century, bow ties started to gain popularity. Back then, men wore black bowties with dinner jackets and white bowties with evening tails.

Today, bowties are frequently used at formal events but are also becoming more trendy for casual attire. A bowtie is your ideal accessory if you like to stand out from your peers.

ways to tie

Start by setting the bowtie face up. Make the necessary adjustments to make the right side somewhat shorter than the left. Here, the right end will be referred to as B and the left end as A.

Move side A on top of B to the right.

Pass A under B, then upwards through the neck loop.

At the joint, fold side B to the right and then towards the left to create a bow shape.

Bring side A downwards and over the middle of the bow shape created using side B.

Fold side A backward to your chest and pinch at the fold.

Push the end of side A (that you are pinching) into the loop now behind side B.

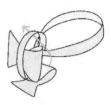

To tighten, pull on the folded parts of the bow.

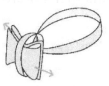

Adjust until you balance both sides of the bow.

CHAPTER 4

DECORATIVE KNOTS

And, of course, knots could also be used for decorative purposes! You'll learn how in this chapter!

Masthead Knot Mat

While this looks complicated, it's easy to make—and is the perfect décor for tables and walls!

Instructions:

1. Make three similar loops.
2. Then, weave two of the outer loops across the center. Do this in an "over and under" sequence, similar to a fishtail braid.
3. Now, thread the end of the rope under and over the middle—across from it—so that the structure could be locked.
4. Follow the path a second time to have it secured.

Ocean Plait Mat

This is perfect as a hot pad or tablet—it's great eye candy!

Instructions:

1. With two long loops, create an overhand knot.
2. Then, twist each loop and have them cross over each other.
3. Get the short end and thread it across the knot to lock the pattern.

Celtic Mat

This is a classic decorative knot, making it interesting to learn about!

Instructions:

1. Thread the ropes in a strict "over and under" pattern.
2. Follow the first round so you can create a perfect Celtic knot!

Fiador Knot

Perfect for lacing curtains and other decors, this one is a treat!

Instructions:

1. On one end of the rope, create an L-shaped loop.
2. Let one end pass through the other end of the loop so you can create an interlocking design.
3. Make sure you hold these loops together and then allow them to pass through the central diamond hole you'll see.
4. Finally, pull the loops away from each other so you can carefully tighten the knot!

Grog's Sliding Splice

Add your favorite embellishments; this knot will catch your visitors' attention!

Instructions:

1. Open alternate strands by using a rod with a tapered end.
2. Then, replace the original rod by adding 6 separate ones.
3. Let the rod pass through one end through the rest of the loops.
4. Attach the end to the main rod and use it!

Wall and Crown Knot

Looking like something your favorite pet could play with, this is quite a convenient item to make!

Instructions:

1. Get the rope and make a noose with it.
2. Then, get the loop and have it tucked into the noose.

3. Now, create another loop, and have it tucked within the previous loop that you have made.
4. Repeat the process, and when you see that the chain is long enough, go and tuck it to end the knot.

Turk's Head

And lastly, here's something you can use to place on the center of the table!

Instructions:

1. Use your hand or a piece of wood to wrap the line with.
2. Overlap so braiding could be started.
3. Braid the end when you reach the third pass, and then hold the loops together. Rotate so you can continue braiding easily.
4. Follow the same path for all three turns, then tuck in the ends to finish.

CONCLUSION

So from all the numerous knot-tying projects that we tackled, I hope you learned a lot from it, and I am glad that you now have the fundamentals of the different knot-tying methods you can do in the comforts of your own home.

Once you have mastered the techniques, rest assured that you can do any knot-tying projects you choose. The projects we tackled are your stepping stone to learning and improving. You can do those projects and others you wish to do with knots in your past.

Also, if you already think that your works are already excellent, you can consider selling for you to earn some money. Knot tying is in demand nowadays because of its stylish look.

The good thing with knots is that they are considered multipurpose, and you can use them to create different accessories that you can wear to add some wow factor to your current outfit.

Knot tying is also a great way to help you to surpass crises because they are very useful and can be a way to save lives, such as if someone is drowning or there is a need to climb very tall places that do not give you access to stairs then this is a great way to reach it just like when there is a fire in the area.

No one knows your personally made accessories might be noticed, and you can earn a lot of money from it. However, if it does not happen, knot tying will teach you a lot of moral lessons, such as:

- It will also boost your creativity, which you can apply in real life.
- Your patience will truly be enhanced simply because tying a knot, especially if the project is a little bit complicated, will require a lot of patience not to get bored.
- It will help you become alert and focus on what you are doing because while tying, you must insert the correct knot on a certain opening for it not to look awkward and unsafe.

So I can advise you to continue practicing to perfect this craft, as it requires a lot of projects for you to get used to the correct knotting for more desirable results. I wish you good luck and success in all your future endeavors.

Takeaway Tips

- Instead of approaching the knots with just one trick, combining them differently is better. Knots are different, and since you cannot say how the knot is tightened, then it's ideal for you to keep trying different tricks.
- If the knot is still very tight, you can try slicing through with scissors or any other sharp object, like a razor blade.

BOOK 3

The Survival Knots Guide (Camping, Outdoor, Bushcraft, Fishing, Hunting)

INTRODUCTION

Knotting is one of those hobbies that will help you relax and survive—whether you get lost in the woods or need ties to keep you safe at home, at sea, and in many more events in your life!

Thus, it's just right that you allow yourself to get the chance to learn how to knot—and guess what? You can learn so in an easy-to-understand manner—courtesy of this book.

From basic knots to decorative ones, scouting, and more—you'll find them all right here! You'll also know how to take care of the ropes you'll be using—so they'll be sturdy and strong and work the way you want them to.

CHAPTER 1

SURVIVAL KNOTS TECHNIQUES

Surviving the Wilderness, the Knotty Way

After calming your nerves and coming up with a plan on how to handle your situation in the wilderness, your plan is likely to be challenged, sometimes because the location you find yourself in happens to have wild animals or the equipment you have do not work well. For instance, you may have a tent, but it got messed up somewhere and cannot stand steady. You may also need to spend your night for your security. What will you do if the trees are tall, slippery, and without much grip?

Using the Taut line Hitch to Steady Your Tent

The Taut line Hitch

You can use a taut line hitch to strengthen your tent, protecting it from being blown off by strong winds.

What, exactly, is a taut line hitch, and how does it work?

The taut line hitch is an adjustable hitch, which you tie on that standing part after securing it around the object. To tie a taut line hitch, you only need to slip the knot to tighten the line, holding it fast under the weight. You end up with a loop knot that is easy to adjust. It is a very useful knot when lines require adjusting, either to loosen or tighten them. You may sometimes hear the taut line hitch being referred to as the *rigger's hitch*; the *midshipman's hitch*; the *tent hitch*; or even the *tent line hitch*.

Ordinarily, when you tie the knot around another object besides the taut line's standing part, you will speak of it as a rolling hitch. Also, when the knot tying is such that the 2nd turn is somewhere between the 1st turn and the standing part, the term adopted is the midshipman's hitch.

This taut line hitch is a popular knot with campers, as they are great for securing tent guy lines. It works so well on tents because it slides freely and can still jam under the load, making it easy to adjust the line as necessary. When *Boy Scouts of America* speaks of the recommended adjustable sliding knot, the taut line hitch is what they are referring to. The important point to take away from here is that if ever you want to adjust how your tent is holding in the wilderness, especially if winds or other weather elements have destabilized your tent, the taut line hitch is the best knot to employ.

How to tie a Taut line Hitch

Begin by turning your line around a post or whatever object you are using, ensuring the place you are tying the knot is many feet away from the free end

Now pick the free end and coil it twice around that part that is the standing line as you work backward in the direction of the post

Next, do some other coiling once around your standing line, and that needs to be outside the coils you've already made

You can now tighten your knot, sliding it on your standing line to adjust the tension.

Some people describe the taut line hitch as two ½ hitches with an additional turn.

The Taut line Hitch Image

Other Sensitive Uses of the Taut line Hitch

If you find yourself in the wilderness with an aircraft that requires tying down.

If you need to climb up trees that are not easy to tackle, probably to keep yourself safe or to have a better view of the horizon

If you want to evacuate from the area and you want to secure loads on whatever carrier you have

Self Rescue Bowline

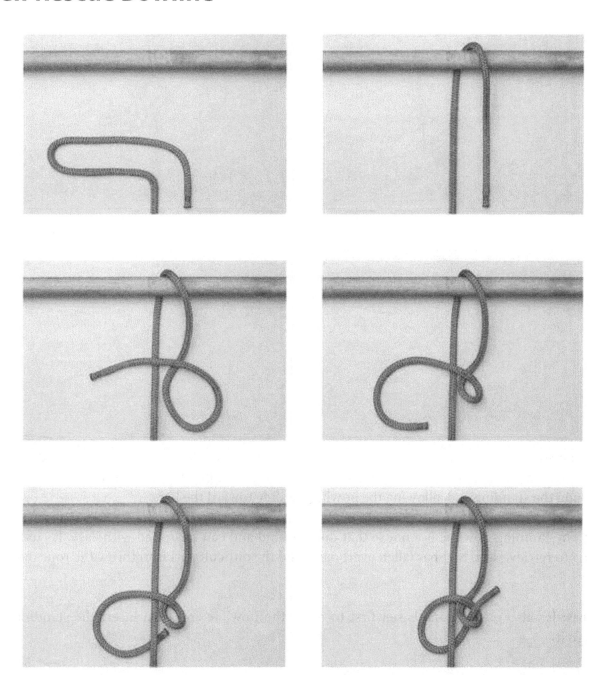

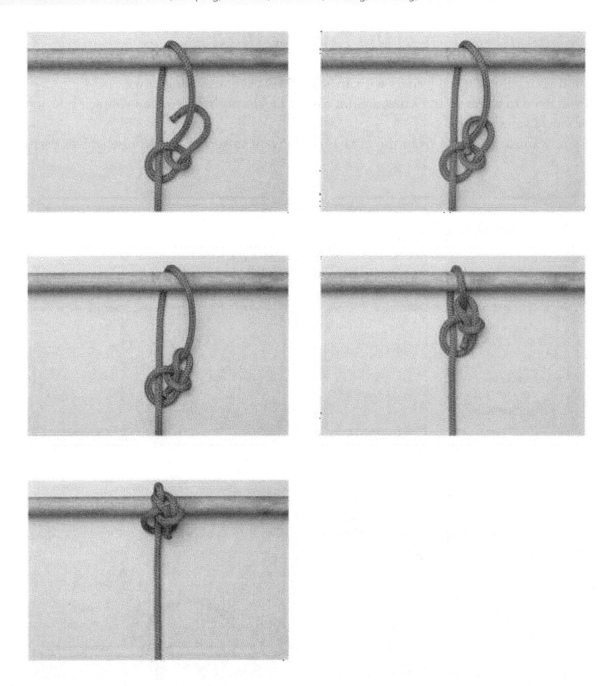

Wrap the string over the bar. Make a bight with the tail. Move the tail around the standing end, through the bight, around itself, and insert it back through the bight to make the bowline. Tighten by pulling the standing end, allowing the bowline to slide toward the bar.

Uses: The Running Bowline is a noose that doesn't bind and can be untied with ease. It's useful in boating to retrieve stuff that has fallen overboard, and the difficult part is to throw the rope over the object.

Choices: It's also possible and easier first to make the Bowline and then insert the standing end through it.

Mastering Ascending Ropes

Do you have some horrible memories from high school gym class in which a middle-aged, pot-bellied gym coach screamed at you to climb a rope? For some of us, the thought of attempting to ascend a rope takes us back to those traumatic days of off-white t-shirts and black gym shorts, but just because you couldn't hack it in gym class doesn't mean you won't be able to do it now.

You were probably not shown the right way to do it. Yes, that's right, your balding, clipboard-holding, whistle-blowing gym coach may not have known the best way to climb a rope!

You see, despite what the old coach may have told you in days gone by, the first thing you need to master when it comes to ascending ropes is to have a sturdy eye splice that will give you good traction as you go up.

And rather than putting the rope between your feet and inching up like a snail, the way you ascend a rope is to grab hold of it as high as you can with your arms, and then while hanging, bring your knees as far up as you can before tightly pressing your feet to the knotted rope.

This is called "braking" on the rope. With your knees up to your chest and the rope tightly held between your feet, now hold your feet in place while you reach up on the rope as high as you can again. To ascend a rope is simply a matter of repeating these steps.

Raise your knees, brake, hold in place, stretch your arms as high as possible, and repeat! You will be a master at ascending ropes in no time! Now at your next high school reunion, you can tell your crusty old gym teacher to put that in his pipe and smoke it!

Learn to Cross Streams and Ravines with Your Rope

So, you are out in the wilderness and come across a raging torrent of a river running directly through your path. What do you do? Turn around, so you don't drown? Well, that might be a wise alternative, but if you have no choice but to cross, you might want to use a rope line to help you cross right over it. How is this done? With a little improvisation, it's quite simple.

All you need to do is lasso your rope to a tree branch or some other sturdy structure on the other side of the water and then tie the other end to another likewise sturdy structure on the immediate side of the stream where you are. As soon as the line is sturdy, hold on to it as you quickly cross the stream.

This little bit of rope goes a long way to ensure you don't get washed away as you make your way across streams and ravines.

Learn How to Make a Gill Net

A gill net could be of great service if you are in a dire survival situation or need good food for the campfire. What is a gill net? It's a knotted rope net that catches fish by their gills! It's relatively easy to make and can be deployed just about anywhere. And the best thing is that once the net is out doing its thing to catch fish, you can cast your attention elsewhere while the net does all the work for you.

The ropes, as mentioned, snag fish by their gills and tangle them up in the netting so they can't get out. After submerging, you can usually pull the gill net out to find a decent catch. To create your gill net, you must take a standard piece of rope and stretch it out from end to end. Attaching each end to a tree would be ideal if you are out in the wilderness, but other stable objects in the environment could also work. You will now need to take another rope and start threading them over the main line you just suspended between trees (or whatever other objects).

You will want to repeatedly wrap the line around in a crisscross pattern employing an "overhand" knot. Next, make tight loops around the "foundation spar" of the rope until you reach the end of your line.

Your gill net is now complete. The best way to use it is to cast it into a body of water such as a river or stream, allowing the current of the water to flow into the net. This will maximize the amount of fish that you catch. Have fun!

Create Your Throwing Rope

If you ever need a length of rope to rescue someone, the best kind to have on hand is a length of rescue rope. This rope can be used to lasso a drowning ocean goer at the beach, or it can be used to help someone trapped in a fire have a new lease on life.

There are many examples in which a throwing rope can make quite a difference in survival situations. Much as the name might imply, this rope is used to alert the person in trouble that you are extending them a literal lifeline.

To create your throwing rope, take a standard piece of rope and double knot one end so that the person you are helping can have a place to put their feet. One final thing to remember when you throw yourself some rope—always try to overcompensate your throw, and give it everything you have when you let loose of that rope so that you know it will reach its intended target. Knowing how to throw rope is one of the most important skills of survival roping to have.

Double Checking Your Harness

This one is important. Even though you may be tempted to think your safety harness is completely secure, you better look again.

Because tragically enough, there have been numerous occasions in which even veteran rock climbers have been deceived by a harness that they believed to be secure, only to have it fail them at some critical moment during their climb. To avoid this nightmare—always remember to check the knots of your harness.

Test Your Knots

This one sort of goes hand in hand with checking your harness. As any rock climber knows, you must check your knots' strength. This means that you need to be sure that the "climber's tie-in knot" is firmly in place, along with an appropriate extra rope backing.

This is all part of testing your knots because the last thing you need is to end up 40 feet off the ground only to find that your knots are failing you! So yes, be sure to test the strength of your knots regularly.

Wear a Helmet

Maybe you like the feel of the mountain breeze rushing through your hair, or perhaps you feel like a bit of a nerd wearing a helmet—well, that's too bad, my friend, because your safety depends on it! Rather than worrying about your appearance, you must worry about your safety and wear a helmet! Any time you risk falling and hitting your head, you should wear a helmet.

Nature may have given us some thick skulls, but they aren't thick enough to withstand an impact from 50 feet up! So you better go ahead and get that noggin covered!

And when it comes to rock climbing, many striking pieces of the head guard are perfectly designed to bring you the cushioning you need to protect your head. Maximizing comfort, convenience, and protection, a proper rock-climbing helmet should fit tightly on your head without squeezing your temples, and it should be tight but still comfy enough to endure the climb. So, wear your helmet, and you will be doing just fine.

Inspect Rope and Belay Device

Your rope and belay device are your lifelines, so you must inspect them carefully and frequently. Be sure to examine the entire length of the rope taking special care to be sure and look for any frayed edges or other signs of damage. As for your belay device, since these mechanisms are essentially used as brakes on your ropes, you must ensure that your rope glides through them quickly and as efficiently as possible. So be sure to periodically pull the ropes through the belay device a few times to ensure they work at optimum capacity.

Make Sure to Keep the Rope Over Your Leg as You Climb

Yes, it's sad but true. One of the number one mistakes new rock climbers make is getting tripped up in their rope line. The best way to avoid this is always to make sure that you keep your rope over your leg as you climb.

This will ensure you don't accidentally get your feet tangled up in the rope as you ascend the rock face. Always make sure to periodically take the time to stop what you are doing, and check your footing to be certain that you are not getting tangled up in the rope as you make progress up the rock wall.

Clip Your Rope Right

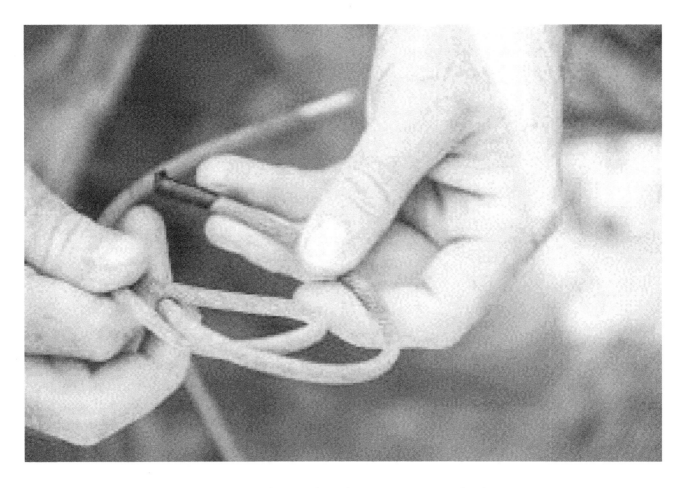

There are occasions in which you might need to clip your rope. To do this, you must reach down to the "tie in" knot on the harness and pull it forward using the full length of rope. Now hold the rope inside your finger and thumb and hook the rope. Finally, push the rope through the D-shaped carabiner of your harness—and let it clip! After doing this, your rope should be in the best position for versatility and strength. These are all great rock-climbing tips to keep in mind.

CHAPTER 2

CAMPING KNOT

Prusik Knot

Known as a "friction knot," the prusik knot consists of two thin cords. To put it all together, tie a rope bundle behind the main climbing cord. After doing this, bring the other half to bear, and use it to create a girth hitch with the knot placed on the outside. Now bring the loop of rope back over the girth hitch and form a "barrel" with the rope's end. Wrap the cord over several times, and the knot is complete.

Adjustable (Sliding) Loop Knots

It is handy to know how to tie an adjustable knot, from tying your camping equipment to a post to creating friendship bracelets.

As much as there is a wide variety of adjustable knots, mastering the slip and sliding knot will provide you with an excellent foundation for every adjustable-knot-tying need.

We will be discussing the different adjustable knots below:

Poacher's Knot

It's also called a double overhand noose, strangle snare, or two-turn (or double) scaffold. This knot is defined as a double overhand knot formed around a bight. Poachers used this knot to catch birds and other equally small wild animals, hence its name.

The poacher's knot is a robust knot that we use to bind an object to a piece of rope, make a simple snare, or join a hand ascender to a foot loop. The unique thing about the knot is that you can make it using slippery ropes like the ones made from Spectra and Dyneema. The strangle snare tends to jam when loaded and becomes problematic to unfasten.

How to tie Poacher's knot

Step 1: Grab the tag end and twist it around a bight of rope.

Step 2: Twist the same end one more time in the same way.

Step 3: Lead the tag end upwards.

Step 4: Slip that end into the 2 loops you had formed.

Step 5: Yank either end to tauten your knot.

Note: Ensure that you don't skip step 2 as most do. When you wrap the tag end only once, you'll form a standard overhand knot which isn't that secure. Also, you can create a stopper knot with the tag end if enough is left for extra security.

Scaffold Knot

The scaffold knot is comparable to the poacher's knot except for an additional turn. It's also known as a triple overhand noose. This knot creates a strong loop capable of slipping, in the same way as a noose, to fit securely around a rail, bar, or similar object.

*When you apply a lining known as a thimble, it can protect your knot against wear caused by chafing - by forming what sailors call a "hard eye". You can obtain thimbles of different sizes from yacht and boat handlers.

How to tie a Scaffold Knot

Step 1: Create a loop at the tail of your rope, then use the working end to make a turn around the standing part and itself.

Step 2: Work back towards the loop you created in the step above to make 3 loose wraps around either line. (Note: if using this knot to secure the loop to something such as a post, start with this step).

Step 3: Once you have completed the 3rd turn, slip the working end into the gaps created by your wraps to run parallel to the standing part.

Step 4: Yank on the working end to secure your knot.

Trucker's Hitch

The trucker's hitch is made so you can have a better mechanical advantage over your peers. It's mostly used to help tarps and the like stay in place and is perfect for surging lines and ensuring friction does not stay strong. It's also known to have an eye at the top.

Instructions:

1. Get the standing end and make a bight right there.
2. After doing so, ensure you tie a Figure 8 Knot in a directional motion.

3. Let the tail pass through the hook you have, and then make sure to pull it tight.
4. Use two half-hitches to tie the knot on top.

CHAPTER 3

OUTDOOR KNOT

Back Splice

The Back Splice is known to have braids on one end and is known to be temporary whipping knots. It's one of the easiest knots you can master!

Instructions:

First, make a crown knot by letting each strand of rope pass through what's next to it and then letting it pass over and under the strands opposite them.

Tighten the knot and let each strand be spliced into the rope by letting them pass under the alternate strands.

Finally, make a second and third set of strands by tucking them at the back of the splice.

Cleat Hitch

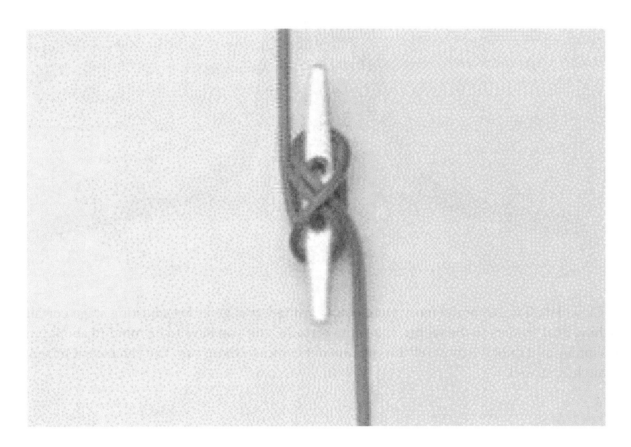

This is used so that a rope can be secured near the cleats and so the rope can pass between the two horns—or the same objects—that you have been using. Because it contains a halyard, you can expect that it will be able to carry some load, which could be quite convenient, especially when you're in the woods. You can use modern elastic ropes, which would work great for this!

Instructions:

Let the rope pass around the middle part of the horn so it could go around the top.

Continue until you reach the middle, and work your way up again.

Then, twist the rope a bit to hook the hitches.

Clove Hitch

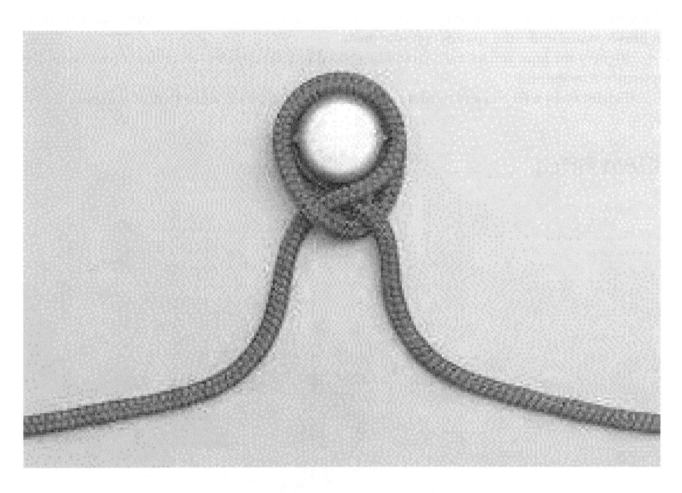

The Clove Hitch is one of the most useful knots around. It is great for adjusting stage curtains or attaching boat fenders to the railing. It is quite versatile, but you have to be mindful about binding and slipping as it's not the most reliable one when it comes to those two. You can have it mixed with half hitches, as well.

Instructions:

Let the end of the rope passing around the pole.

Please continue to do so until you reach the standing end, and do it around the pole.

Finally, make sure to thread the end of the rope under itself and then pull it tightly so you can create this knot.

Coil Unattached Rope

Adjustable Grip Hitch

Common Whipping

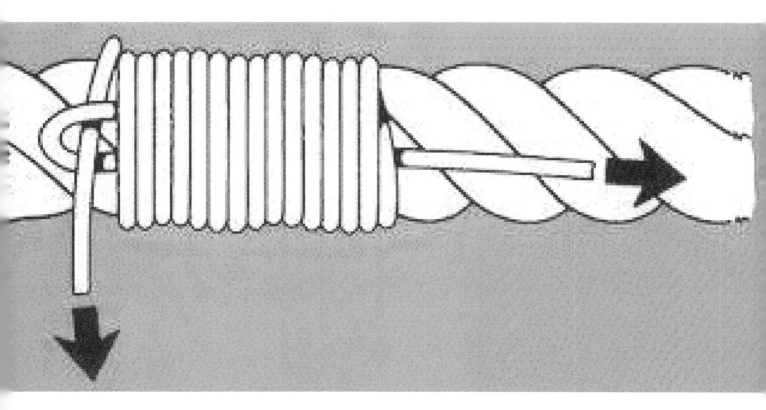

This is usually knotted near the rope's end and has different variations, especially when caring for the bight. If the end of the rope has already been melted, it's just right that you use the common whipping. This also has an almost invisible exit point, making it one of the neatest knots! However, you have to ensure that none of the strands unravel because the whole knot will be distorted when that happens.

Instructions:

Place the twine near the rope by laying it there.

Get the long end of the rope and wrap it 8 times around the rope.

Once you have reached the 8th turn, let the final turn pass through the first bight you have created.

Then, pull the short end of the rope so you can have the long one secured before trimming the ends off.

Twisting Constrictor

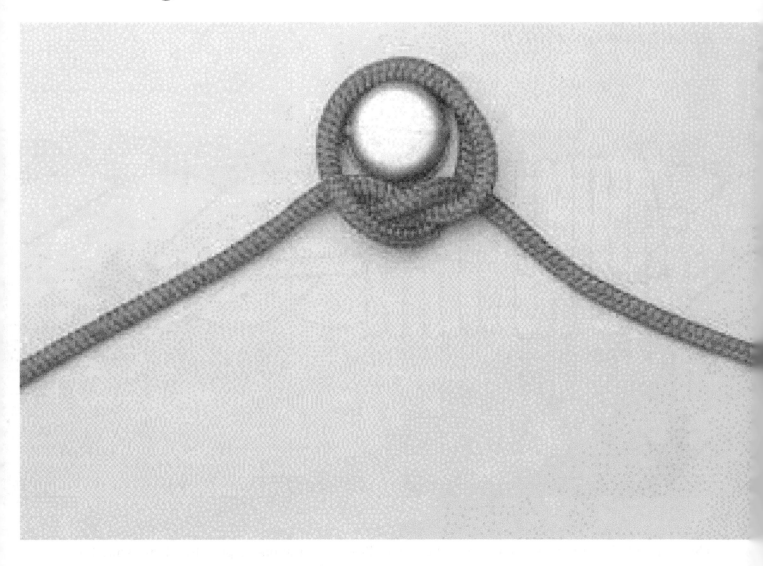

The Twisting Constrictor has a good whipping mechanism and is perfect for securing bags or sacks. Sometimes, it is also used as a hose clamp and can glue certain items together—or at least hold them close to each other. You can also fray a rope's end with the help of this knot.

Instructions:

First, twist the rope so you can form a Figure 8.

Fold down the loops until you reach the center to form the knot.

Eye Splice

Perfect when using synthetic materials, the Eye Splice is an alternately knotted material that allows you to do many things. One thing you must remember, though, is that you have to secure the ends with tape or heat—by burning them with a candle—so that you can be sure that there are around 3 times of unraveling that could happen. This works under various circumstances, so you're in for a treat!

Instructions:

First, tape or heat the ends of the rope.

Then, unravel at least 4 to 5 tucks of it.

Arrange the strands of the rope before letting them pass through the center of the standing strand.

Let one pass lower than where you have first let the other rope pass under the adjacent side of the standing strand.

Continue doing so for the rest of the strands, then remove the tape before using.

Farrimond Friction

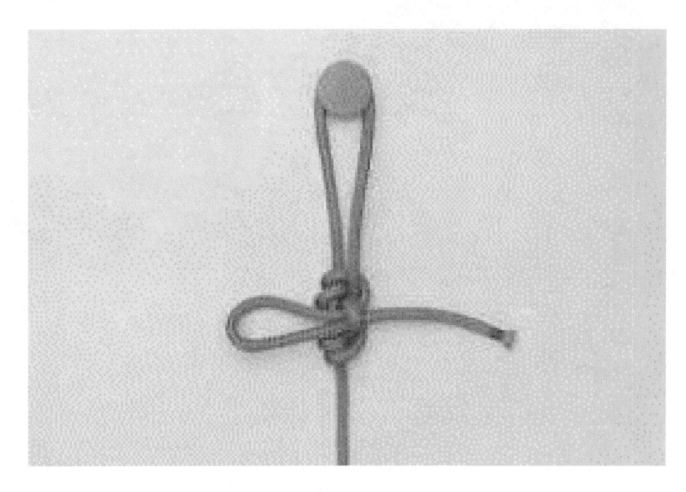

This type of knot provides a conveniently quick method for tightening ridge lines of tents simply by pulling the end of the hitch. Friction becomes effective for this knot, which is why it was named as such.

Instructions:

Let the end pass around the branch or the tree.

Then, make a loop and wrap it around the rope's standing end twice.

Finally, make sure to tuck a bight at the end of the loop so that you can have it tightened.

Square Lashing

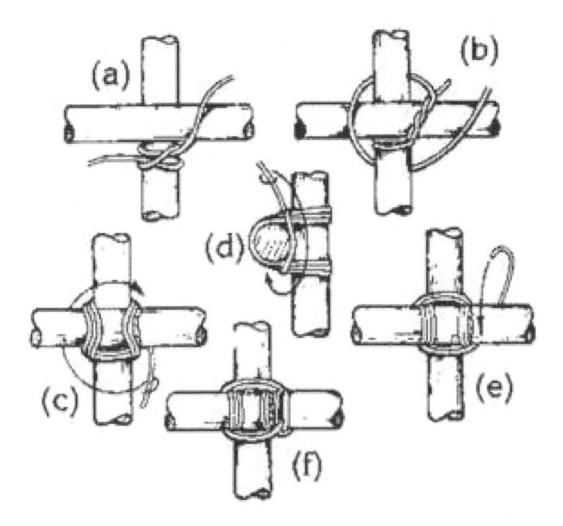

This knot could make it easy to bind two poles together and ensure strong scaffolding. It's the kind of knot that allows you to make support frames or helps you lash through the sides of trees. With this knot, you can also wrap some ropes around a stick while bending your knees and pulling them tight with your legs!

Instructions:

First, make a clove hitch on one of the poles. Let the clove hitch wrap around the pole.

Then, twist one short end, and wrap it around both poles. Do this around 3 to 4 times.

Now, you must tighten the lashing and repeat it 3 to 4 frapping times.

Lastly, end the knot by making 2 to 3 half hitches. Make sure that they are tight, so they are secure.

Diagonal Lashing

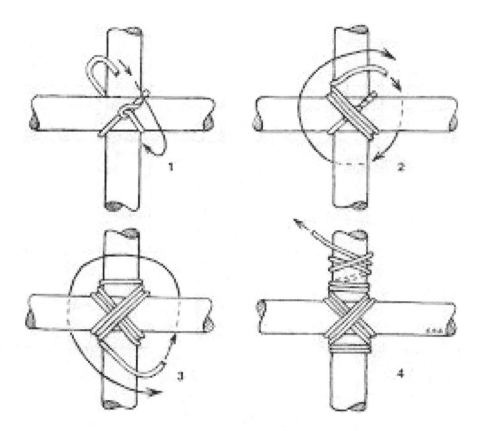

A different version of the Square Lashing could also hold poles together but in a diagonal manner. You could also add the timber hitch to close gaps or tighten your poles to the ground so you'd be safe!

Instructions:

First, make a single timber hitch, then wrap them twice or thrice around the two poles, and do so only in one axis.

Follow the first axis with the other one.

Now, have the lashing tightened by making 3 or more frapping turns.

Use a clove hitch for the ending.

Round Lashing

The Round Lashing is mostly used for lashing two parallel pieces together. Why? So you could make a longer unit, of course! If you're having problems with the security of this knot, make sure that you'd hammer the edges so they can be wound together tightly.

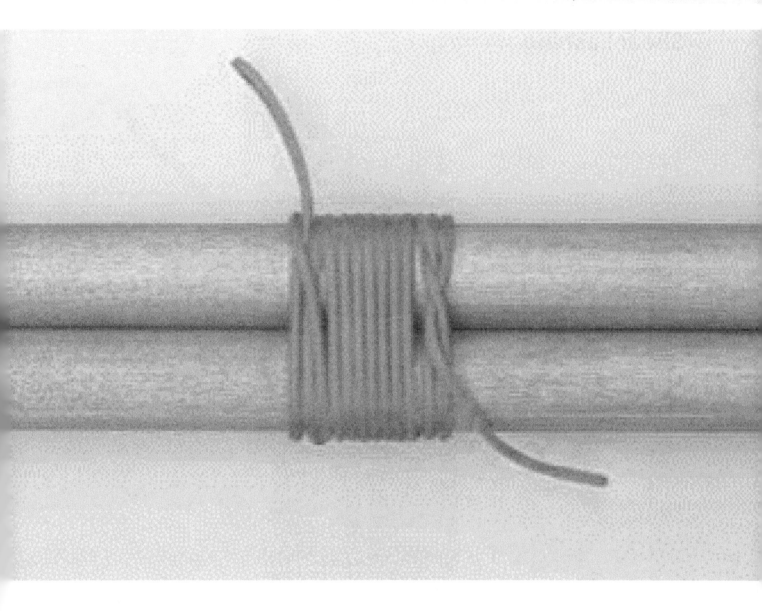

Instructions:

Make a clove hitch first. Do so around the two poles.

Then, wrap the rope at least 6 to 8 times around the poles.

Make another clove hitch to finish the knot.

If you make two, your pole will be longer!

Shear Lashing

Shear Lashing works for poles laid side by side next to each other because the ends are held not just by the shear lashing but also by the round lashing. If you're having problems with security, it is best to remember that you can hold them as tightly as possible while standing near the pole.

Instructions:

First, tie a clove hitch around one of the poles.

Then, use a simple lashing to wrap both poles.

Now, make 2 to 3 frapping turns to wrap the lashing.

Use a clove hitch to tie the ends, and spread the poles together, as well.

Tripod Lashing

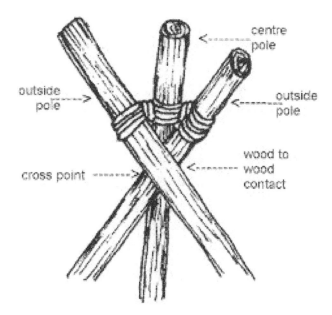

Tripod lashing allows you to pass between two to three poles, especially when using frapping turns. You also have to let the center pole extend towards the opposite direction and ensure not to wound everything too tightly as it would affect the quality of your lashing. Remember that trial and error is important here—so don't be so scared of making mistakes!

Instructions:

First, make a clove hitch around one of the poles.

Then, wrap at least 6 racking turns around three of your poles. Weave them in and out to do so.

Now, make 2 to 3 frapping turns. Do so in the gaps between the poles.

End it with a clove hitch, and cross the two poles outside so that the tripod lashing can be completed.

Shear Lashing

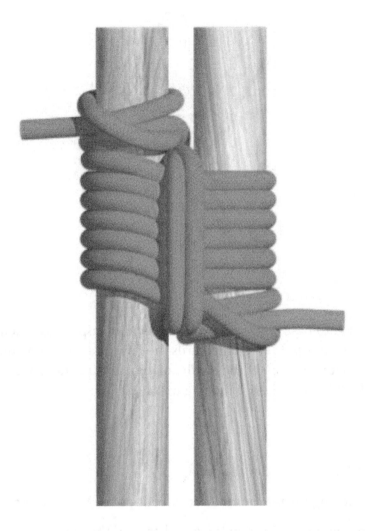

It is also called "sheer lashing, " called 2-spar shear lashing. It's used to bind together 2 spars that are parallel, which will then be stretched out from the parallel position to create sheer legs. In the same way, we form an A-frame. This lashing involves taking frapping twists in the middle of the poles and tying a clove hitch around just one of the legs.

How to Tie a Shear Lashing

Step 1: Begin by tying s clove hitch around one pole.

Step 2: Make 6 wraps before starting the first frap.

Step 3: Create 2 fraps in the middle of your poles.

Use a clove hitch to secure the loose ends, then finish the lashing by separating the legs.

CHAPTER 4

BUSHCRAFT KNOT

Overhand Knot

The overhand knot is one of the most common knots tied by people. It's usually used for tying two ropes together and can be used as a stopper knot to prevent the rope from going through other objects, such as turnbuckles or grommets. If you are tying a boat to a dock, it can also be used this way. Overhand knots are also used to secure a life preserver onto a person and can be tied very easily, but they are often tied incorrectly if they are not tied in the right place. The overhand knot is often tied by using the thumb and forefinger of one hand and pulling the loop down over two fingers of the other hand.

Half Hitch

Half-Hitch

Two Half-Hitches

The Half Hitch looks like the knot has been tied with the rope's end passed through the object so you can secure it.

Instructions:

First, make a loop around the object.

Let the end pass through the loop and the standing end.

Tighten the loop so you can form a half-hitch. Please do it again so you can make two half-hitches.

The Reef Knot

Besides its obvious use in fastening shoelaces and belts, the Reef Knot has many other applications. It is best employed when it joins the ends of one line to hold an object in place, where such fastening is not intended to be permanent. It is also used often in macramé and, as mentioned earlier, for securing bandages and slings. It is also commonly used to tie garbage bags.

Although easy to tie, the Reef Knot is not known for its strength. As such, it can be used as a general-purpose binding knot, but it should only be employed when tied so that the completed knot lies snugly against the surface of whatever it is securing. Under no circumstances should the knot be used in place of a bend, as it will give a false impression of strength before quickly unraveling. In addition to this, it should never be used in a situation where reliance on it places life in balance. The International Guild of Knot Tyers has endorsed this viewpoint. Some sources claim that the failure of Reef Knots when employed in the wrong situations has been responsible for more deaths than all other knots.

Lastly, it should be noted that Reef Knots work best when tied using the opposite ends of either the same or similar lines; if there is any difference between the lines in terms of texture, thickness, or stiffness, this will weaken the knot considerably.

How To Make A Reef Knot:

STEP 1

Taking the two ends of your line, place the end on your left (End A) over your right (End B).

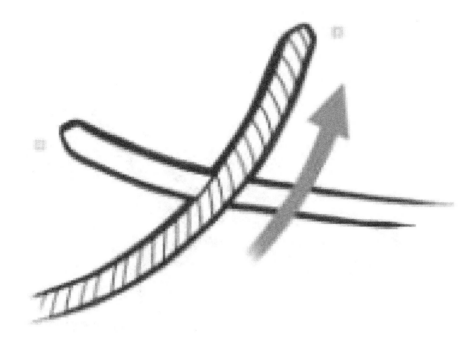

STEP 2

Take End A under and over the standing part of End B. Take End B over and under the standing part of End A.

STEP 3

With both ends pointing upward, cross End A over End B. Take End A under and then over the standing part of End B. Bring End B over and then under the standing part of End A and pull to tighten.

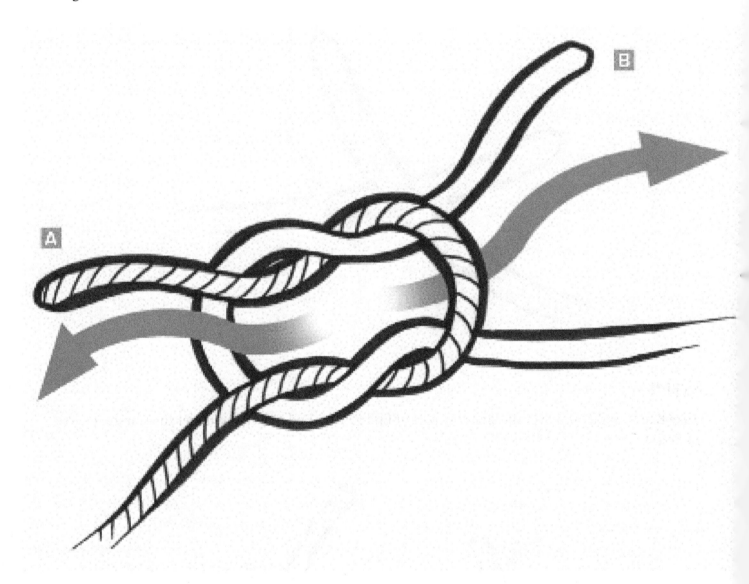

The Strangle Knot

Strangle knot is a Binding or Double Overhand knot great for keeping multiple objects together with a rope that goes at least once around the objects and can secure the neck of a sack. It is also quite similar to a constrictor knot, but the main difference between them is that Strangle knot's ends go at the outside edges, and with the constrictor knot, they go between the turns.

How to make the Knot:

1. Go with the rope around the bar and cross it with the first turn.
2. Pass the rope again, going in the same direction.
3. Tuck the rope under the first, turns, and makes sure to tighten them strong enough.

The Bachmann Knot

The Bachmann knot is a friction hitch that requires a round cross-section carabiner. Arborists or hikers mostly use it. The knot finds the best use when the friction hitch needs to be constantly or quickly altered, but it's also easily made self-tending, so we can say it's multi-practical. The hitch is easily released by grabbing the carabiner while unloading, sliding, and moving up or down when needed.

The best use is the locking carabiner for the Bachmann knot since you will take it to move the hitch. Moving the hitch is done by unclipping the top loop and releasing the cord. If you are using a non-locking carabiner, to ensure the knot is safe, it is best to use it with the carabiner gate facing down. That way, it will have much less chance of unclipping itself.

How To make the Bachmann Knot:

1. Make a band of rope or put a pre-made tie into the carabiner.
2. Wrap the strop around the rope while holding the carabiner against it, and then pull the strop through the carabiner.
3. Repeat the action once more if there is a space in the carabiner.
4. Put the load at the bottom of the strop so the knot is at the friction point.

The Poacher's Knot

A Poacher's knot (also known as a variation of the Double Overhand knot) is a very secure knot that can be used to create the foot loop to a carabiner, or cavers can use it in making a cow tail. It is a very safe hitch knot. Poacher's knot can be made out of horsehair though it is hard to imagine using that material nowadays.

How To make the Poacher's knot:

1. Start by creating a bight at the bottom of the rope.
2. Not so tight. Wrap its end around that bight two times.
3. Complete the Poacher's knot by pulling its end through those turns.
4. Tighten the knot firmly.

The Common Whipping Knot

The Common Whipping knot is a typical whipping knot or several knots tied at the bottom of the rope to prevent the end from loosening, and its advantage is that it can be tied without using a needle or any other tool. The Common Whipping knot is easily tied and secure, with no visible ends if correctly tied. Its disadvantage is that it can slide easily off the rope's end if any turns get cut. Since it can slide, it is best to use this knot with natural fiber rope and natural twine than the synthetic one because it will hold it at the rope's end and prevent it from unraveling. Again, if used with synthetic rope, it is best to wrap it with tape to avoid slipping.

How To make a Common Whipping Knot:

1. Put the twine along the rope.
2. Create a bight back on the rope.
3. The rope is supposed to be whipped near its end.
4. Firmly wrap the twine around the rope and the bight of the twine.
5. Continue wrapping until the whipping is double as wide as the rope.
6. Wrap the working end of the twine through the bight.
7. Slowly pulling the twine's standing end will get both the bight and working end under the whipping.

CHAPTER 5

FISHING KNOT

Double Fisherman's Knot

The Double Fisherman's Knot lets two ends of a line come together and is one of the best stoppers around, especially if you'd use Technora or Spectra Rope. It's perfect for load-bearing mechanisms and could work as full-length rope abseils to help you easily retrieve the rope. It may seem not easy, but it's definitely the opposite—and you could easily learn how to make it!

Instructions:

Let the loop pass through the rope, strap, or harness.

Then, thread it to the other end of the strap, and let it lie neatly before pulling it tight.

Albright Knot

Fishermen frequently need to join one line to another of larger diameter or to connect the solid braided wire to a fishing line. The Albright Knot has served this purpose well for more than fifty years. It is not only a serviceable knot but is also an attractive one when completed. While it performs fairly well with braided gel-spun lines, there are better knots, such as the Huffnagle Knot, for this purpose.

When connecting one line to another with a larger diameter, it is best to make a Bimini Twist in the lighter line before building the knot if maximum strength is desired. If connecting the solid wire to a fishing line, it is best to construct a Haywire Twist in the wire and then flatten the wire loop before making an Albright. Otherwise, the wire under pressure will sometimes slither through the Albright, allowing the fish to escape.

Step 1: Form a horseshoe shape in the larger line to be attached to the line from the reel. (If the solid wire is used, make a Haywire Twist loop instead of the horseshoe shape.) Insert the tag end of the line inside the horseshoe shape or wire loop as shown.

Step 2: Squeeze the horseshoe shape together and, working left to the right, make at least twelve turns with the tag end of the line around the two strands of the heavier line or wire loop. Be careful not to overlap any of the strands. If an overlap occurs, the line will sometimes break. After the wraps are made, insert the tag end through the U of the horseshoe-shaped heavier line or wire loop, as shown. Note: Both ends of the line should now be on the same side of the U in the heavier line.

Step 3: Tease the coils close to the end of the U. Be careful not to slide them over the end. When closing the knot, it is important to pull firmly on the tag end of the line first, preventing the coils from

unraveling off the heavier line. Then pull on the main line, bringing all the coils together snugly. Finally, pull on the tag end again to close the knot as tightly as possible.

Step 4: To lock the knot, make six half hitches around the main line with the tag end so it won't come loose. Tease the half hitches down until they are firmly closed against the Albright. This will lock the knot securely.

Step 5: Clip the two tag ends close to the knot.

Tip

Once a knot has been securely closed, any protruding ends should be clipped flush. Dangling ends can tangle a leader's tippet. On smaller flies, dangling tag ends spoil the appearance and performance of the fly on the retrieve.

Arbor Knot

Fishing expert Bill Nash of San Jose, California, has created a method for securing the backing line to the fly reel spool that provides 100 percent line strength.

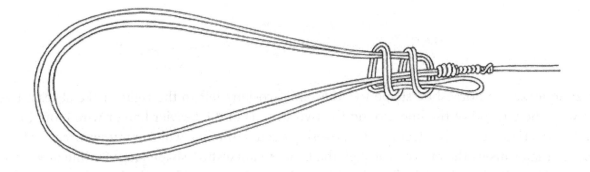

Step 1: Make a loop at least 24 inches long by tying a Bimini Twist at the end of the backing line. To ensure 100% strength using a gel-spun line, build a 70-twist Bimini or add a drop of Loctite 406 to the Bimini. Create a loop with the doubled lines that end in a two-turn nail knot. Use one hand to hold the loops and the other to tighten the nail knot.

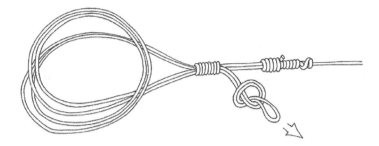

Step 2: Create an Overhand Knot after the loop, tease it against the Nail Knot, and then tighten. Reduce the end.

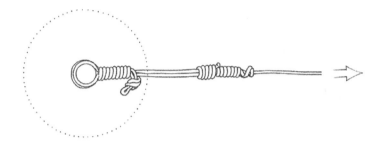

Step 3: Pass the double loop over the spool rim and onto the reel arbor after removing the spool from the reel. Pull on the main line to make the loops on the shaft tighter. The main line might need to be worked back and forth to close the loops completely.

Tip

100% Knot

A 100% knot has the same strength as a line with no knots. A poorly made knot weakens the line, and the line becomes weaker as a knot slips.

Australian Braid Knot

Not only is it useful, but it's also easy on the eyes, too! The Australian Braid is surely one of the best knots you can make because it is easy and quick to tie. Use at least 6 to 50 lines, with 1 to 8 inches braids, respectively.

Instructions:

Make a loop but leave a long tag near the end.

Then, braid the loop, make sure you've lightly tagged the end together, and then use the bight to pull the original loop in.

Now, lubricate the loop and tighten it by tagging on end smoothly.

Trim the ends of the tag to complete the knot.

Tighten the knot and trim.

Bimini Twist Knot

One of the most widely used knots for tying two pieces of line together for optimal strength is the Bimini Twist. If the knot is properly tied, it won't budge, allowing the line to operate fully. You can make a knot with the two strands of the Bimini by using the two legs of the loops, which guarantees a very strong knot.

The Bimini Twist works well in monofilament and fluorocarbon lines, but Dacron and contemporary braided gel-spun lines don't perform as well. Making 20 twists in the loop has been the standard for many years. If only twenty twists are produced, that's acceptable with monofilament, fluorocarbon, or Dacron lines, but Bimini Twists created with braided gel-spun lines tend to slip under strain. Most seasoned fishermen concur that you should complete the Bimini Twist with fifty to sixty twists on braided gel-spun lines. With braided lines, securely tie the knot with a drop of Loctite 406 to prevent the Bimini Twist from failing.

To make a shock absorber, you can add twists to monofilament or fluorocarbon lines. When fishing with very light lines where a rapid jerk could break off a fighting fish, building 50 to 60 twists in mono before finishing the Bimini allows the knot loop to expand like a rubber band.

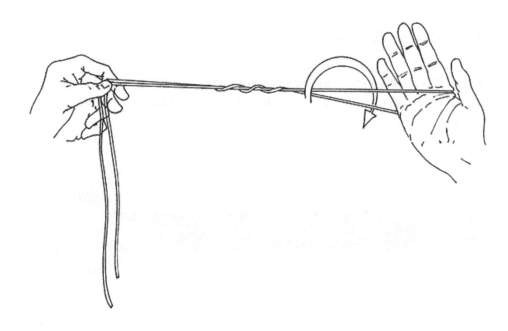

Step 1: Pull off enough lines to make the desired Bimini Twist. Grasp the tag end and the main line firmly with one hand, making a loop. Slip the other hand inside the loop and make the desired twists.

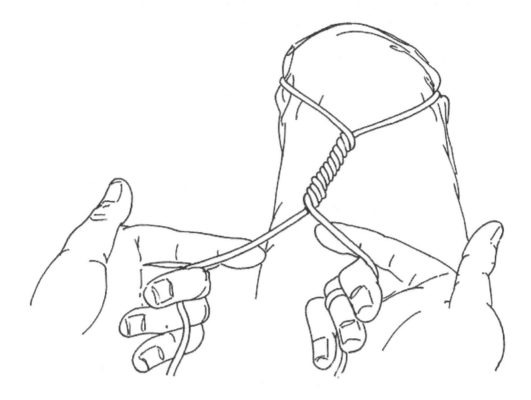

Step 2: Slide the loop over your knee, making sure the knee is bent at less than a right angle to prevent the loop from slipping off. Grasp the main line with your left hand and the tag end with your right, and slowly and evenly spread them apart, forcing the twists toward the knee. Continue until the twists touch your knee. This will ensure that the finished loop will have even twists throughout.

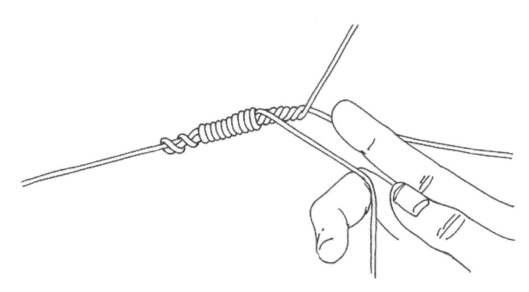

Step 3: Keeping both lines taut, move your left hand to the right until the main line is straight and parallel to your body. The tag end must be positioned with your right hand just above a right angle to

the twists. Keep your right hand inching closer to the twists while keeping the tag end taut. You may get the tag end to start rolling around the twists by slipping your finger under the loop and starting to push upward. The initial two spins around the twists must be spiraled to achieve the knot's maximal strength. The turns should then be spaced closely after that.

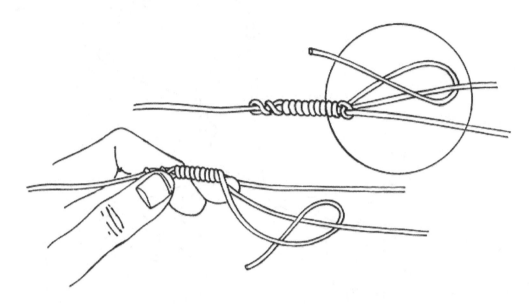

Step 4: While keeping tension on the main line, creep your left hand up to pinch the wraps and trap them. Now with your right hand, make a half hitch with the tag ends around one leg of the loop and then another half hitch on the other. This is especially important with braided lines so that when the line is being strained, the two legs of the coil exert even pressure in a knot.

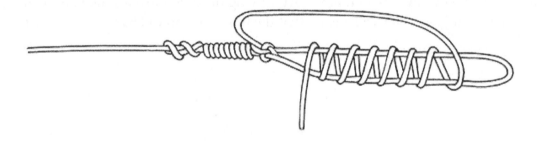

Step 5: Use the tag end to make six turns around both legs of the loop.

Step 6: After you have made six coils with the tag end around the two legs of the Bimini loop, place the tag end, so it lies alongside the main line and is at least an inch past the Bimini. Pinch the main

line, the Bimini, and the tag end in one hand, and with the other hand, grasp one leg of the loop and make five turns around both legs of the Bimini loop, being sure to position each of the turns tight against the Bimini. This removes the twists created by turning the six coils around both legs of the Bimini loop, often making closing the knot difficult. The loop is now free of twists.

Step 7: Continue to pinch the Bimini and the turns around the two legs and then grasp the tag end and pull firmly on it to close the loop and the knot.

Blood Knot

The Blood Knot (often called the Barrel Knot) is a popular method of joining dissimilar strands of monofilament or fluorocarbon lines. It is most frequently used to build tapered leaders for fly fishing. The Blood Knot consists of two Clinch Knots, which is not recommended for braided gel-spun lines.

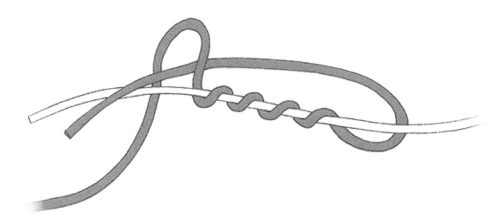

Step 1: The tag ends should be placed across each other on the major lines, and you should wrap one tag end around each main line in succession. Only three revolutions are advised when testing lines that weigh more than 25 pounds. As the line's diameter gets smaller, make more turns. Make six revolutions with the smaller line, for instance, when the line's test weight is less than 8 pounds.

You may now address a potential issue when creating the remainder of the knot. Form a loop with the active main line in front of the first turn, as seen in the step one example, and pinch it with your thumb and finger to keep it in place. Insert the active tag end through the loop between the active main line and the second tag end after completing the necessary twists around the line.

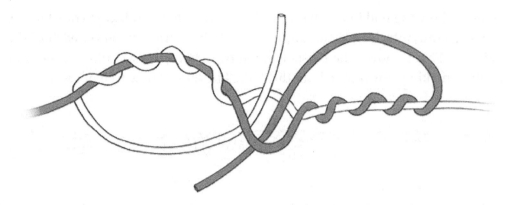

Step 2: Continue to hold the loop with your thumb and finger. Now take the second tag end and make the required number of turns around the other mainline as shown. Then insert the second tag end down through the loop between the two lines. Carefully hold the loosely formed connections with both hands and place them between your lips. Gently pull on both main lines, allowing the twist to form the knot.

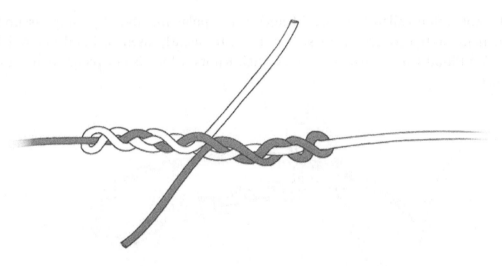

Step 3: Remember that any Clinch Knot can be difficult to close properly unless all strands lie against the spirals. This is accomplished by gently pulling on each tag end until the formed knot looks like the illustration for step 3.

Step 4: Lubricate the knot and slowly but firmly pull on the two main lines to seat the knot correctly. Trim the tag ends flush.

Tip

A nick significantly reduces the strength of a monofilament line. You should examine the line after landing a fish or if you think it may have been nicked. Put the monofilament between your thumb and first finger to accomplish this quickly. When your thumb is forced into your finger, apply pressure to the monofilament. Continue pulling the line while pressing the mono firmly against your finger; you will feel it if there is a nick. After landing a large fish, it is always a good idea to trim the leader close to the fly, discard any pieces that came into contact with the fish, and then reattach.

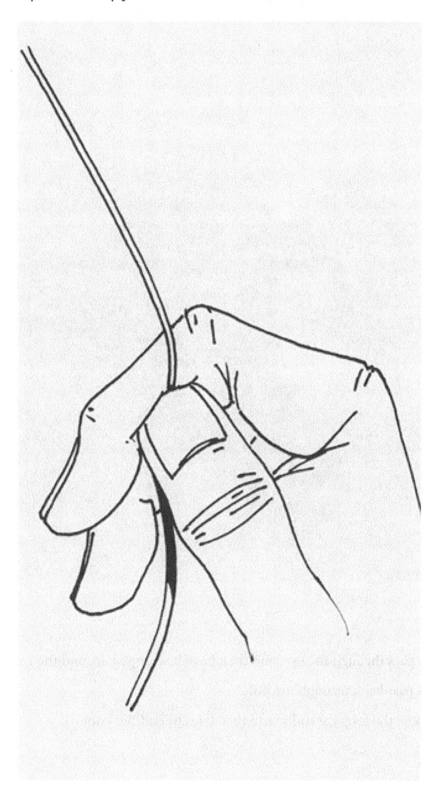

Davy Knot

This knot has been used since the 1950s when the Welsh Fly-Fishing Team has been experimenting with fishing knots. It's quite economical and portable—mostly because it's small but reliable!

Instructions:

First, let the tippet pass through the eye, and then have it wrapped around the running end.

Now, let the tippet pass back through the hole.

Tag the end to tighten the loop carefully, and then trim to end the knot.

Slim Beauty Knot

Slim Beauty is a relatively new knot that has acquired popularity among fishermen worldwide. One of the best knots for joining a fluorocarbon or monofilament line to a shock or bite leader of the same weight or greater strength.

One can tie the Slim Beauty knot quickly and easily. A Slim Beauty tied to a heavier bite or shock leader with a single mono strand without using a Bimini Twist results in an extremely compact knot. When using a casting plug or spinning tackle with a mainline less than 15-pound test, and you wish to connect a longer, somewhat heavier length to this line before connecting to a lure or bait, this knot is extremely useful. I like to use a 6- or 8-pound-test line for targeting smallmouth bass, but I frequently add two or three yards of 10-pound-test mono as a long shock or bite leader.

Step 1: Make a Double Overhand Knot in the heavier line (shock or bite leader).

Step 2: Slowly pull on the two ends until the knot resembles Figure 8.

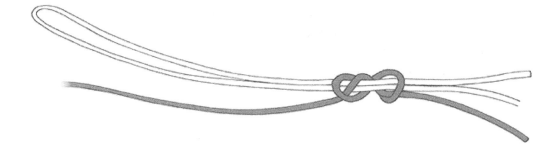

Step 3: Double the thinner strand to form a loop about 18 inches long. Insert the single-strand loop straight through both loops of Figure 8, as shown. After wetting the knot, close the Figure-8 Knot firmly with pliers.

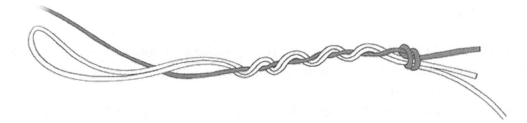

Step 4: Make four wraps with the doubled lighter line around the heavier shock or bite leader. The number of wraps is a personal choice. Some anglers believe four wraps are enough, while others think six to ten are better.

Step 5: Then wrap the loop back over the first wraps three times toward the Figure-8.

Step 6: Insert the end of the loop through the gap between the Figure-8 Knot and the first wrap made. Wet the wraps around the shock or bite leader, or you may have trouble closing the knot. Do not pull on the end of the doubled loop to tighten the knot. Grasp the heavier line firmly (gripping it with pliers often helps) and pull on the single strand (main line). This will slowly cause the wraps to form like a Blood Knot as they are compressed toward the Figure-8 Knot. Make sure no coils overlap.

Step 7: Once all wraps are against the Figure-8, firmly close the Figure-8 and pull as hard as possible on the main line to complete the connection. Trim the ends of the loop and the tag end of the heavier shock or bite leader.

Egg Loop Knot

The Egg Loop is perfect for catching fish and shrimp by making fish roe as bait! It's useful and one of the best things you could learn!

Instructions:

First, let one end of the leader pass through the eye.

Now, wrap the long end of the rope around the hook 15 times until you reach the short end.

Let the long end pass through the hook to create a loop.

Wrap some more until you have let the loop go around 7 times.

Now, pull the long end of the rope so that the egg loop can be used!

Accessories And Tools for Fishing Knot

Hooks

The most popular method of fishing and the one most used by recreational anglers is hook fishing. It is almost impossible for most people to catch fish without a hook. With the hook method, you will need a fishing hook and all the other accessories that make the hook work.

Various hooks can be used in fishing, but they all serve the same purpose. A hook is simply a J-shaped metallic line used to tangle the fish. There are single, double, and circular hooks; for beginners, single hooks are the ideal and recommended option.

The size of the hooks also varies. Those looking to fish bigger fish should go for bigger hooks, while those looking to catch small fish should try the smaller ones. When purchasing hooks, look at the hook numbers. The numbers on the hooks are inverse to their size in relative comparison. The smallest hook is size 32, while the largest is size 19.

Fishing Rod

Everybody knows a fishing rod, even those who have never tried fishing. A fishing rod is a long, flexible pole used to cast a fishing line. The fishing rod is an important part of the entire process since it works as part of the fishing technique.

Fishing Reel

Fishing rods work hand in hand with fishing reels. The reel is attached to the rod to help cast the line and wind it up to bring out the catch. Without the reel, it would not be easy to bring fish onshore.

This especially applies in cases where the catch is too big and may overpower the angler. In this case, the reel supports the fish being brought out of the waters.

Fishing Line

You know you will need a line to catch fish with your hook. Ideally, there are no other means of hook fishing unless you are using a line. Some reels you purchase from the market may already come with a roll of line. However, it is advisable always to carry one or two more rolls off the line just in case yours gets tangled in the waters. It is common for fishing lines to get tangled, banned, or fall into the water. That's why you must always have extra.

Fishing Bait and Lures

Once you have your hooks, line, and rods, you want bait or a lure. Without baits and lures, attracting fish to the hook is impossible. Ideally, bait is placed on the hook to draw fish to it. The fish follow the bait to eat it and are tabled on the hook when they try to grab the bait and swallow.

There are different types of baits and lures. You attach Bait at the end of the hook to attract the fish. The best option is live bait since they are more attractive to fish. The common live baits used by anglers are worms and minnows. As we have already discussed, minnows are small-sized fish that can be caught in the water or purchased at a bait store.

Besides worms and minnows, other commonly used baits are corn, grubs, smooshed bread, and marshmallows. These foods can be placed on the hook to attract fish to a feast.

Bobbers

Bobbers are small round floaters that help keep the bait closer to the surface. They also help you notice when a fish is interested in your bait. This is because the bobber is visible to you and not the bait. In most cases, the movement of the bobber alerts you that the fish is trying to attack your bait.

Sinkers

Fishing hooks are very light in weight, and most hooks may not even sink on their own. This is the reason why sinkers are needed. Sinkers help stabilize the weight on your line, making it possible to sink the hook. Ideally, one sinker is enough to be used on one hook. However, never carry just one sinker when going fishing. I recommend having several sinker boxes since they can easily get lost.

Swivels

When you get into the waters, you will realize that some baits and lures make the line spin which makes it twisted. The line may get tangled and difficult to handle due to the spinning. You can stop it from spinning by using a swivel. The swivel works as a connecting tool between your line and bait and allows the bait to spin and not the line.

Line Cutter

You will need a sharp line-cutting tool. You may want to cut a line if it is tangled in debris or if you wish to combine two lines to attain a certain length. You may also have to cut extending ends after tying a loop.

There are many types of cutters from which you can choose. Ideally, any small cutter tool that can fit in your pocket could work as a cutter, and I normally use my nail cutter. You can also use a penknife or similar objects available to you. You can also purchase a special line cutter tool from a local fishing gear store.

Tackle Box

The tackle box is a small box where anglers store their tools. Tackle boxes vary in size depending on the number of tools used. For instance, most beginner anglers only fish across the shore. For this type of fishing, having a huge tackle box is unnecessary. You can carry a small box with bobbers, swivels, and sinkers. However, for those fishing in deep waters, say in the middle of the lake, it is necessary to have a bigger box. This is because you will need a lot of tools, such as hooks and sinkers. You may also need some extra lines and even a reel. This makes it possible to continue fishing even if you lose some items in the water.

CHAPTER 6

HUNTING KNOT

Flat Overhand Knot

The essential knot is the regular overhand knot. This is presumably the knot that almost everyone naturally knows how to tie. It can be used as a plug knot; however, different knots are tied by first making an overhand knot. For instance, when you tie an overhand knot around an item, for example, a tree, shaft, or grommet, it is known as "a half knot."

As you read, you will see that tying an overhand knot is a common step in major knot-tying procedures.

Pros: This knot is very easy to tie.

Cons: Depending on the kind of rope used in making this knot, it might become hard to unclasp if it is put under overwhelming pressure. This is normally when the knot is made using extremely slender cordage.

Step-by-step instructions for tying:

Make an overhand loop as shown below

String the working end up from underneath the loop as shown below

Pull the working end and the standing part to fix the knot, as shown below

Potential Uses:

1. A few knots may slip when a heap is encountered. Placing an overhand knot toward the end of a rope can help keep the knot from pulling apart when there is weight or tension on it—hence, it can be used as a "plug knot."
2. If you have a rope you are attempting to clutch but with accompanying stress, you can prevent the rope from slipping by tying an overhand knot.
3. If you balance a tarp to set up a rain cover, an overhand knot tied toward the rope's end can keep the rope from sliding through the grommet on the tarp. Feeding the rope's standing end through the grommet and the overhand knot will prevent the rope from sneaking past the opening when you join the working end to a tree, rock, or stake. If the rope is long enough, the knot won't simply move past the opening you string it through.

Clove Hitch

Considered one of the most important knots for a camper, the clove hitch is a fast and efficient means of lashing poles—and just about anything else—together. For example, if you are out camping and need to quickly lash a few sticks together before you throw the tarp over them as a makeshift shelter, the clove hitch would help make this possible. The knot is fairly simple to assemble, and with a little repetition, most can quickly tie it up with a single hand.

Before you begin, one thing to remember is that the clove hitch knot isn't 100% secure and tends to come loose with everyday wear and tear. For this reason, the clove hitch is often recommended for temporary holds until a sturdier knot is placed. Furthermore, the clove hitch can be made more sturdy by putting a stopper knot at the end of it.

This one needs a pole to get started, so as mentioned in previous sections, and application is similar to the closet rod in previous sections. First, wrap the rope over the pole, then pass it over the "standing part", with the crossing end placed over the other. Now place the crossing end under so that it is in line with the other end. Next, start tucking the termination point diagonally underneath the knot.

Now carefully pull out the "working end" and the "standing part," keeping the general formation of the knot as you do so. Keeping the working assembly stable is key before you tie the final knot. If you can do this, you will have a stable structure to utilize the rest of your rope length. Finally, tighten everything up, and the clove hitch is complete.

CONCLUSION

At first glance, knot-making may seem like one of those strange niche hobbies that only people with a lot of time on their hands would be interested in. But this couldn't be farther from the truth. Knot-making is a vital skill that could save your life in a true survival situation.

If you were stuck out in the wilderness and needed to get safely from one ledge to another, a well-knotted rope could be the best thing in your arsenal. Also, if you need to lug up some heavy items, a knot such as a barrel knot will give you that capability. In short, if you ever find yourself in a precarious situation, you might find nothing quite like a good knot!

FINAL WORDS

Thank you for reading this book!

Hopefully, you've learned something about knotting—and are now ready to make your own.

Follow the steps featured and take care of your ropes the way you should, and you'd have a great time with this hobby.

Finally, if you have enjoyed this book, please post a review on Amazon. It will be greatly appreciated.

The word 'knot' stems from the Old English cotta meaning 'knot, tie, a noose.' Knots are everywhere and are an amazing resource for sailors, mountaineers, campers, and other adventurers. They help people trap fish, hold tents, and even assist first responders in building emergency shelters.

But knots don't just exist in the outdoors. Knitting enthusiasts have been using them for centuries to craft everything from sweaters with intricate stitches to breezy summer tops that keep you cool while you watch the sunset. Some can take days to master, but once you know how to tie a knot, you can create anything from lace collars and decorative cuffs to dainty lanyards for keys or necklaces. A knot is an older tie representation, and the ancient Egyptians used knots to secure material around support or other objects before wrapping it with string.

For most applications, each knot is sufficient to secure the rope. However, more complicated structures are needed for stronger bonds in ropework or when three-dimensional structures are required.

Knots are not just useful in life; they are an important part of many daily tasks. Various knots can be employed, from tying down cargo to attaching one end of a rope to another. You might even need them for your household chores. If you're a traveler, you probably have a few knots for rope and tie or untie knots in your back pocket.

Many different types of knots can be tied using these methods; the key is that they all use the same method.

Made in United States
North Haven, CT
20 December 2024

62934655R00096